BAN
THIS!

BAN THIS!

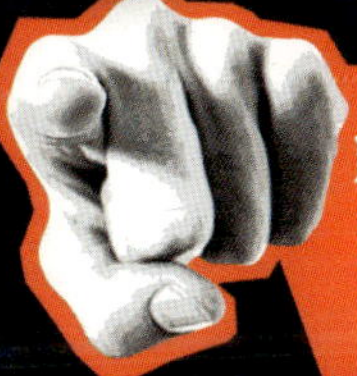

HOW ONE SCHOOL FOUGHT TWO BOOK BANS AND WON (AND HOW YOU CAN TOO)

CHRISTINA ELLIS / RENEE ELLIS / EDHA GUPTA
BEN HODGE / PATRICIA A. JACKSON / OLIVIA PITUCH

Zest Books™
An imprint of Lerner Publishing Group, Inc.
241 First Avenue North
Minneapolis, MN 55401 USA

For reading levels and more information, look up this title at www.lernerbooks.com.
Visit us at zestbooks.net.

Designed by Kimberly Morales.
Main body text set in Univers LT Std.
Typeface provided by Adobe Systems.

Library of Congress Cataloging-in-Publication Data

Names: Ellis, Christina, author. | Ellis, Renee, author. | Gupta, Edha, author. | Hodge, Ben (Theater teacher), author. | Jackson, Patricia A., author. | Pituch, Olivia, author.
Title: Ban this! How one school fought two book bans and won (and how you can too) / Christina Ellis, Renee Ellis, Edha Gupta, Ben Hodge, Patricia Jackson, Olivia Pituch.
Description: Minneapolis : Zest Books, 2025. | Includes bibliographical references and index. | Audience: Ages 11–18. | Audience: Grades 7–9. | Summary: "*Ban This!* equips readers with arguments against the common reasons that are given to ban books in schools and public libraries. Having successfully fought against book bans in their school district by organizing protests and media interviews to raise awareness, the authors share how to fight back against book bans, speak out against censorship, and win the right to intellectual freedom" —Provided by publisher.
Identifiers: LCCN 2024020291 (print) | LCCN 2024020292 (ebook) | ISBN 9798765629970 (library binding) | ISBN 9798765629987 (paperback) | ISBN 9798765639108 (epub)
Subjects: LCSH: Libraries—Censorship—United States. | Libraries—Censorship—United States—Case studies. | Challenged books—United States. | Children—Books and reading—United States. | Teenagers—Books and reading—United States. | Multicultural education—United States.
Classification: LCC Z711.4 E45 2024 (print) | LCC Z711.4 (ebook) | DDC 025.2/13—dc23/eng/20240609

LC record available at https://lccn.loc.gov/2024020291
LC ebook record available at https://lccn.loc.gov/2024020292

Manufactured in the United States of America
2-1013802-52303-12/3/2025

I'd like to dedicate this book to my family who supports me through every adventure and advocacy passion. I want to dedicate this book to my father, Mario C. Ellis, who always puts my sister, Renee, and me, before himself. I love you, Dad, with all my heart. And to my Grandpa, Fernando Ellis Jr., who passed away shortly before this book was written. Thank you, Grandpa, for being with us to your last breath. Until heaven, we shall meet again. And most importantly, thank you, GOD, for giving me the courage and strength every day to fight for a world of peace and justice. —C.E.

Thank you, GOD, for this opportunity and for Your mercy and grace. To my dad, Mario Ellis, who has sacrificed so much and always pushed and encouraged me to become the best version of myself. To my mother, Deborah Ellis, who will always be a light in my life. To my grandmother, Barbara Ellis, who has prayed for me throughout my entire life. To my sister, Christina Ellis, who will forever be my partner in crime. And in loving memory of my grandfather, Fernando Ellis Jr., who always listened, encouraged, prayed for me, and poured into my life. Last but not least, much love to my cousins and family! And to all my lovely, crazy, yet beautiful friends, I thank you for your support and the priceless memories we've shared over the years! —R.E.

Thank you to the unwavering support of my friends and my family in helping me to believe the power of my voice. To my mother, who was there as a rock for me in the late nights and who selflessly loves me. To my sister for teaching me what it means to stand up for myself. To my father, who shows me what true sacrifice, hard work, and leadership looks like. Thank you to my friends, who are my cheerleaders. This is for you. —E.G.

To Shahida Muhaimin for showing me the way and my partner, Jenn, for keeping me in the fight. —B.H.

To the kids of the Panther Anti-Racist Union who saw something wrong and stood up for what was right. —P.J.

Thank you to my books, giving me access to worlds and experiences I didn't know existed. Thank you to music for teaching me how to harness my voice. Thank you to the outspoken generations for fighting the hard battles. Thank you to my friends and peers who have always stood by my side. Thank you to my family for providing me with unwavering support and love. Thank you to my mother, the strongest woman I know, for raising me to be the fighter I am. This is to all the children of the future who deserve representation, diversity, and compassion. —O.P.

CONTENTS

TIMELINE OF THE CENTRAL YORK SCHOOL DISTRICT'S FIRST BOOK BAN

JUNE 2020	The Panther Anti-Racist Union (PARU) is formed at Central York High School (York, Pennsylvania).
JULY 2020	Educators in the Central York School District compile a list of resources (books, videos, worksheets, etc.) that can be used for teaching about diversity and multiculturalism. This list is made available to all educators in the district.
AUGUST 10, 2020	Some school board members challenge the list at a board meeting and propose removing the items on the list from the schools.
SEPTEMBER 21, 2020	PARU leads first rally protesting the board's actions, gathering students and members of the community who call for diversity in educational resources.
OCTOBER 5, 2020	PARU leads the second community rally.
NOVEMBER 2020	The board bans the materials on the resource list, but the superintendent does not enforce the ban.

AUGUST 2021	The local news reports to the community about the ban.
SEPTEMBER 3, 2021	PARU students plan protests and demonstrations.
SEPTEMBER 7–10, 2021	PARU holds a three-day protest in front of the school.
SEPTEMBER 13, 2021	PARU holds another community rally, asking the board to reverse the ban.
SEPTEMBER 14, 2021	PARU members are interviewed by CNN for *Don Lemon Tonight.*
SEPTEMBER 16, 2021	A community member organizes former CYSD alums to support PARU. Raises $2,800 for the club by October 2021. All the money is spent on providing books to members of PARU and to create an anti-racist library in one classroom.
	PARU organizes book read-alouds from the banned resources list.
SEPTEMBER 17, 2021	PARU continues to protest in front of the school.
SEPTEMBER 18, 2021	PARU meets with Pennsylvania State Representative Malcolm Kenyatta.

SEPTEMBER 20, 2021 PARU holds another protest in front of the school in preparation for the board meeting later in the day. Their main cry is "Reverse the ban!"

PARU participates in another community protest later that night before the board meeting is held.

The school board votes to reverse the ban and reinstate all of the banned resources.

NOVEMBER 2022 A single parent in the school district files a secret complaint to the Central York High School administration, demanding the removal of the books *Sold, Push,* and *A Court of Mist and Fury* from the school library. The complaint is sent to the new superintendent.

DECEMBER 2022 The superintendent forms a secret committee that votes to ban the books using a policy meant for curricular books, not library books.

MARCH 6, 2023 A conservative Facebook group called Take Back Our Schools PA celebrates *Push*'s removal by a CYSD parent. This is the first time anyone in the district hears about this.

MARCH 14, 2023 PARU organizes and responds to the second ban by posting on social media, wearing red, and speaking once again at board meetings.

MARCH 27, 2023 Sapphire, the author of *Push*, sends a statement to the board, read by Patricia A. Jackson (see the appendix).

MARCH–APRIL 2023 PARU speaks at board meetings and conducts several press interviews to protest the new ban. The district once again wavers and defends their position.

MAY 5–JUNE 5, 2023 PARU votes to begin protesting outside of school each morning from 7:00 to 7:30 a.m. These protests go on each morning for one month.

JUNE 12, 2023 After almost two months of protests and activism by PARU, public scrutiny, and the press force school officials to once again reverse this ban. A new policy is crafted, saying that no one parent or community member can remove a book for the whole school anymore. They can only opt their own child out. The policy passes.

INTRODUCTION

PRECISELY AT THE POINT WHEN YOU BEGIN TO DEVELOP A CONSCIENCE, YOU MUST FIND YOURSELF AT WAR WITH YOUR SOCIETY.

—JAMES BALDWIN

The story of the Panther Anti-Racist Union (PARU) of Central York High School is one born of necessity, an essential need to create and hold safe spaces for children of color when none were accessible to them. In June 2020, it was a bold move, considering the rise of racism and hate crimes after the 2016 election and the upheaval in the wake of George Floyd's murder. But it was a gamble that paid off, allowing children of every walk of life to unpack their frustrations in an effort to help them be understood and help others understand where they were coming from. The best life lessons are taught by those who are unaware that they are teachers. This was one of the purposes of the club.

The Central York School District encompasses a suburban and industrial swath of country in south-central Pennsylvania. Known for Harley-Davidson, Caterpillar, and a plethora of defense contractors, it is a deeply red zone, known for its conservative beliefs. From 2008 to 2020, it had one of the fastest-developing populations of diverse people in the county because the district was on the cutting edge of diversity and inclusion training. People wanted to bring their children to the district.

But PARU's purpose would make a dramatic shift from the creation of safe spaces for kids of color to the preservation of our school community and democracy itself. As Baldwin suggests, we became embroiled in a war against a small segment of society that wanted to revise American history by erasing the achievements and even the existence of people of color and members of the LGBTQIA+ community.

In July 2020, a group of well-intentioned educators came together to decompress about the racial reckoning sweeping the nation in the wake of Floyd's murder. The core of our purpose as teachers is children. We were concerned about the questions students might bring back to school when the district resumed session in August.

We compiled a list of resources: coloring books to picture books, *Sesame Street* videos, and documentaries on the works of Jane Elliott and James Baldwin. These resources were meant to help educators open a dialogue with their students. We never imagined that this list would become a lightning rod for right-wing conspiracists. Key members of the school board, urged on by a small but vocal group, accused the educators involved of being indoctrinators and subverting the district curriculum with critical race theory. The teachers, who sought to answer a need for our population, were also called unpatriotic, Marxists, and Communists.

Members of the board of school directors lobbied to have every item on the list banned. So, PARU went from being a safe space to air grievances to a full-blown, student-led activist group. We could see no one was coming to save us. We had to save ourselves.

In November 2020, in the midst of the COVID-19 epidemic, the school board voted unanimously to enact one of the largest book bans in American history. Reading about the ban in the local newspaper, members of PARU took their next steps to becoming full-blown activists. With guidance from administration to ensure they were adhering to school rules and not disrupting the educational process, they planned and orchestrated a campaign that included a social media barrage and strategic on-campus protests.

For eight weeks, the club members chanted and held signs outside the school. Parents honked in support. Other students joined in. Administrators gave fist bumps in the hallway. The media came calling. Before anyone knew what was happening, PARU's activism was picked up by the local, national, and international news. Essentially, our school community was ground zero for the rising storm of censorship plaguing public schools and libraries.

After initially doubling down on its decision, the school board changed course and voted unanimously to overturn its own ruling and reinstate the books, delivering a

The second generation of Panther Anti-Racist Union who led and pushed back against the first of two book bans in Central York District. *Back row, left to right*: Christina Ellis, Renee Ellis, and Ben Hodge. *Front row, left to right*: Olivia Pituch, Edha Gupta, and Patricia A. Jackson.

win for PARU and the Central York School District. Across the country, other student organizations such as Diversity Awareness Youth Literacy Organization would use the model of PARU to create their own organizations to fight back against the threat of censorship.

This was just a battle. The war was far from over. Only two years after the book ban's defeat, a new school board would attempt a second, smaller book ban. In a dry run of a new censorship tactic, they would remove three books from the high school library under the guise of parent challenge and parental rights. A new wave of PARU students would be there to meet them head-on. After much media attention, the second book ban was defeated.

PARU's initial purpose was to claim space for kids, help them to find their voice, and grant them courage for speaking their truth. But in the fire of confrontation, the club's protests forged these young people into outspoken activists who could not only tell their story but also could uplift and carry the voices of other marginalized people.

What you'll find throughout this book are the arguments the book banners used to justify their actions and the *counterarguments* educators and students created to fight the ideas the book banners were putting forth. You can read the book from cover to cover or select individual chapters that may represent the issues you're currently facing. We want this book to serve as a resource for teachers and students who may be facing their own book bans. We hope others can learn from the strategies we developed and unite against forthcoming waves of book bans and other attempts at censorship.

We did it. Twice. And so can you.

—The Authors

CHAPTER 1

IS THERE A RACE PROBLEM?

Patricia A. Jackson, co-adviser of PARU

Beginnings are important. In just about every aspect of life, beginnings tell us where we came from, track how far we've come, and measure how far we need to go. With every beginning, there is a catalyst—a spark that marks a jumping-off point onto the journey. For me, that catalyst was May 25, 2020, when George Floyd was murdered by law enforcement in full, uncensored view of the nation.

I felt bitter and inconsolable, consumed by a fury that had no place to go except inward. Another Black man was dead at the hands of the police, who were supposed to protect us. Unlike many people who lifted their voices in protest, I wallowed in silence, believing my voice held no weight. My mother told me there was nothing I could do about people like the ones who had killed Floyd, except pray for them. This frustrated me. My mother, who grew up in a segregated South, also believed that the Reverend Martin Luther King Jr. was an instigator, not a peacemaker. I had been raised to bow my head and accept what came to me in silence, even acts of abject racism. Fortunately, I am my father's child, and there is only so far a human can be pushed.

During the summer of unrest that followed the highly publicized murder, I received an email from a fellow teacher inviting me to a discussion with a group of school counselors and teachers in the district. Our intent was to talk about how Floyd's death might affect our student population, particularly children of color. While I appreciated the sentiment, I knew the outcome, and I warned them that this work

An aerial view shows a memorial area in honor of George Floyd in Minneapolis, Minnesota, on May 24, 2024.

would receive racist backlash from certain members of the school board. The majority of my colleagues were white. They didn't get it, but they would soon learn the kind of racism people of color experience daily. For pointing a finger to Floyd's murder and asking Americans to do better—to be better—they would find themselves on the receiving end of racist ideologies. With the purest of intentions, the group proceeded anyway. Despite the storm that would come, I had to accept that invitation. Being a teacher isn't a job for me; it's a calling to a higher purpose.

A clenched fist memorial sculpture at the site of the 2020 killing of George Floyd by a police officer in the Powderhorn neighborhood, south of downtown Minneapolis.

When we first met, we were a group of a dozen teachers and school counselors from across the district—elementary, intermediate, and secondary—who pooled our expertise and experience to compile a list of picture books, age-appropriate fiction and nonfiction, websites, online materials, and other resources to review and share among ourselves to prepare for student questions about Floyd's murder. There was even a video from *Sesame Street* in our list. Our intent was to assist our peers to pivot away from the violence and focus on how our diversity unites us.

We saved these resources in a Google doc online that was initially shared between us. Once the list was compiled, our group planned our next steps: speaking with our building administrators. Many principals were delighted with the initiative we had shown, the purpose, and the work that went into compiling the list. They urged us to push it up the chain of command to the superintendent. He shared our enthusiasm and commitment. Since 2007, the Central York School District had been on the cutting edge of diversity in the county. He wanted to share our work with the school board. On his recommendation, the Diversity Committee arranged a series of subcommittees with administrators, board members, educators, and community members.

In late July 2020, no more than two or three sessions after the Diversity Committee convened, our educator group got wind that the school board was unhappy with our list of resources. A member of our educator group, an elementary teacher who was instrumental in compiling the majority of the titles, was listed as a "red flag" teacher, or one who needs to be monitored for their behavior, by some members of the board. I remember a curdling sensation in my gut. I had warned my fellow educators that our work would not be met with enthusiasm. But the trouble that we had unleashed on ourselves was far more heated than I'd expected. The response from two particular board members was loud, immediate, and frankly racist! These white women objected to our curated resources and started making noise about the removal of the books as well as the removal of the teachers who had created the list.

They accused the teachers of secretly stocking the books in classrooms and adding these resources to the curriculum. They demanded the list be released to the public for review. The vitriol stirred up by these board members on social media got so volatile that teachers began removing their names from the shared list out of fear for their jobs. The owner of the document, for her safety, turned ownership over to the superintendent. Without a thorough vetting of the resources on the list by people qualified to do so—teachers—the board's talk of banning the entire compilation became a hot topic of discussion on social media.

A newly elected board member, whose children had been homeschooled until she ran for the position, said the following when the school board convened for the first time in August 2020: "Do we even have a race problem here?" Her question spoke to her privilege and would lead to one of the largest book bans in the history of the United States.

This remark became a mantra that would drive the board's agenda. If you say something enough, the sentiment becomes truth to some people. This is just one of many false-bottom arguments the board would use to support their book ban. In what many community members called an overreach of their powers, the board would ban every listed resource from school libraries and classrooms, seize newly written curriculum for subjects from math to social studies for their *private* review, and investigate any teacher who spoke up about these actions.

This stance and the arguments that followed aligned with the talking points of right-wing organizations such as No Left Turn in Education and the Heritage Foundation. The school board stood firm in their acceptance of white supremacist tenets and used them to try to silence PARU and discredit our protests. Because they could not openly attack the students without facing backlash from the community, the board moved into a smear campaign against the teachers who provided books to students by authors of color and LGBTQIA+ authors in their classrooms.

No Left Turn in Education and the Heritage Foundation are far right-wing organizations that promote conservative ideology.

To complicate matters, one board member encouraged her friends from a homeschooling network to escalate tensions with nuisance complaints against teachers. By filing right-to-know requests, they hoped to find evidence of wrongdoing by teachers and collusion with the superintendent. They also hoped to bog down the district in paperwork—a tactic referred to as paper terrorism. Their goal was to intimidate teachers to keep them from speaking up or fighting back against the book bans. It worked—with one exception: the advisers of PARU and a handful of teachers who came to stand at the protests.

Board members would take jabs at the faculty during school board meetings and accused teachers of indoctrinating students to hate the police, their families, and religion. Some parents who monitored social media bought into the belief that teachers were white-shaming their children or making them feel guilty about historical interactions with people of color. Employing the same fear-mongering tactics she'd used on the public via social media, the school board's loudest antagonist convinced her fellow directors to vote for a ban. She wanted the entire list of resources—by or about people from marginalized backgrounds—removed from every district school and every classroom library. On November 10, 2020, the board of directors voted unanimously to do just that.

The African adinkra symbol Hye Won Hye. It is a symbol of imperishability and endurance.

Over three hundred titles were banned. Everything from children's books such as *All Are Welcome, Pink Is for Boys,* and *Not Quite Snow White* to such videos as *I Am Not Your Negro,* a docudrama about the life of James Baldwin. They banned a coloring book of African adinkra symbols and a PowerPoint presentation by a former student, Niema Abdullah, about how to increase minority student participation in SAT testing and Advanced Placement courses. The board also wanted a memo sent to every teacher in the district to enforce the ban. But the superintendent refused to comply with their wishes.

Led by their newly elected director, a homeschooling advocate, the board of directors embarked on a campaign of suppression, disguised as parental concern. After the resources were banned, the school board tabled for more than two years the curriculum for social studies over alleged concerns of critical race theory. The homeschooling advocate believed that the superintendent, who had no part in the curriculum rewrites, was inserting critical race theory, Marxism, and reverse racism into the curriculum to demonize white people.

Any initiatives centered on social justice, social-emotional learning, or diversity, equity, and inclusion became synonymous with being anti-Christian, anti-family, anti-police, anti-government, and anti-white. When a community member said that LGBTQIA+ people were "unconstitutional" and a danger to her child, the board sat in silence.

As a secondary teacher, I was unfamiliar with most of the elementary titles on the banned list. So, I went to the bookstore to read them for myself. What I found were books filled with children of color, Muslim kids, queer kids, and disabled kids with uplifting messages of acceptance and hope. There was no critical race theory on the colorful pages. No hate speech. No reason for white kids to feel ashamed or guilty. The book ban's purpose became clear to me: suppress and erase the life experiences of people of color and LGBTQIA+ people.

PARU has always maintained a strong stance against book bans and supported our perspective with positive, affirming arguments whenever we spoke in public. In 2022 we shared our story at the Reimagining Education Summer Institute at Columbia University in New York. As a result, our interview with CNN correspondent Evan McMorris-Santoro was broadcast on *The Don Lemon Show*, and we spoke on the *At Liberty* podcast of the American Civil Liberties Union (ACLU). Here is how we responded when asked "Do we even have a race problem?" or "Are the books being banned filled with critical race theory?":

FIRST

Yes, we *do* have a race problem.

When we, as a society, fail to teach our children empathy, they may cross the line of cultural propriety and may believe they are entitled to do so, even at the expense of another person's dignity. This sense of entitlement creates *microaggressions*, such as self-segregation, where children of color will avoid certain sports, student clubs, high-level classes, and even performing arts for fear of being singled out or mistreated.

Microagressions are comments that may be unintentional but are demeaning to a group, that simmer beneath the surface and can erupt in unexpected ways.

The saying that "kids will be kids" can create an excuse for racism and misogyny. Until calling a Black person the N-word became a hate crime, our school handled it by giving the offender detention or letting them off with a warning. "They didn't mean anything by it" was really just an excuse for racist behavior. But at whose expense?

I had a Chinese American student named Bao. White students, primarily boys, thought it was funny to say, "Take a bow, Bao" whenever this student did well in class. I wanted to intervene, but Bao asked that I not interfere. But one day, I had enough and sternly reprimanded the boys.

Instead of calling the boys out, I called them in. I explained the disrespect they were imparting. That by using Bao's Asian name to reference a culturally Asian practice they were engaging in racism, even if they felt it was in jest. They didn't have his permission or the right to disparage him or his identity, and continuing to do so was offensive. Good fun turned to alarm and ignorance to understanding. I'll never forget the looks on their faces. They weren't upset by my scolding; they wanted to make amends for offending a well-liked peer. They apologized to Bao and shook his hand. After class, Bao thanked me. There was no recurrence of the behavior—in or out of the classroom. Teachable moment. Lesson learned. That's a win!

SECOND

Critical race theory is an academic concept taught in higher education (usually law school) that suggests race is a social construct, an idea that has been created and accepted by people in a society.

Critical race theory is based on certain inequitable aspects of society that are embedded into our social order, giving some people an unfavorable advantage, especially in the legal system. It is neither a course nor a concept taught in high school and definitely not taught in K–8. The accusation that critical race theory was being taught in our school was a *dog whistle* meant to mislead and fire up parents, making them believe that their children were being subverted.

A dog whistle is the use of coded or suggestive language in political messaging to garner support from a particular group without provoking opposition.

The school board attempted to redefine patriotism and what it meant to be American by painting teachers as Marxists or Communists during the board meetings. Old dog whistles from a bygone era but still effective. They had no evidence. While they condemned the faculty, not one director had ever visited my classroom to see what I did daily. The only way to beat this was to be present where they wielded power—at the meetings—and show them who the teachers really were.

None of them knew about the half dozen students who chatted at my door every morning, the students who came to my room during lunch to avoid the chaos of the cafeteria, or the kids who hung out in my room during my planning period. They didn't know about the students who came to me, not to be "indoctrinated" with critical race theory but because I was an adult who listened and empathized with the traumas and dramas of growing up.

Yes, there is a race problem at our school, and it's a systemic one.

WHAT TO SAY

When faced with questions about whether talking about race or the concept of critical race theory is appropriate for kids, respond this way:

- **Race problems are everywhere, in attempts to ban books by marginalized authors and in the daily microaggressions that chip away at self-esteem and identity.**
- **Critical race theory is an academic concept taught in higher education and does not appear in texts for younger readers.**

CHAPTER 2

WILL SOCIAL-EMOTIONAL LEARNING DAMAGE AND TRIGGER KIDS?

Olivia Pituch, secretary and social media adviser of PARU

Social-emotional learning (SEL) has been in schools for over twenty years. SEL programs encourage children to treat others with empathy, with compassion, and the way *they* would want to be treated. The concepts of embracing differences, celebrating cultures, and demonstrating empathy toward others are far from new in a classroom. Despite this, banning books has been "backed" by the claim that education should not teach social-emotional learning. The people who were calling for book bans at our school suggested that reading books or facilitating discourse about hard subjects will damage and trigger kids. To counter this idea, we made the following arguments:

FIRST

Reading about their own experiences can help students feel validated and seen.

Personally, I have found that reading about experiences that both differ and align with my own has helped me grow. When I read a book that mirrors events I have had to work through, I feel validated and seen. Too many kids feel alone in the world, and it's easy to assume no one understands what you're feeling, so to read your thoughts written by someone else is comforting.

I have faced abuse in my life. In college, we were assigned a book that was from the point of view of a character being abused. I talked to my professor, letting him know the book might be a hard read for me. He understood and assured me he would provide an alternative if needed. If my feelings got too heavy, I could simply walk away from the book. As I began to read, however, I was overwhelmed with how understood I felt by this character. She was putting feelings I never knew how to describe into words and writing all the things I never had the courage to talk about. Before I knew it, I had devoured the book, feeling a new sense of empowerment and validation.

After some light digging, I found that I am far from the only one with this experience. "Mirror books," or books that align to a reader's own experiences, have been shown to "provide validation and affirmation, tell students that their stories matter and show students possibilities of who and what they can be." Minority groups already have limited options to validate their experiences. Mass media usually perpetuates white, male culture, with the book bans mainly silencing LGBTQIA+, female, and BIPOC voices. Book bans prevent minority groups from receiving the validation, affirmation, and empowerment that mirror books provide.

I have found it just as impactful if not more to read books and explore experiences that differ from my own. Diverse books educate and spread awareness, but they also can increase empathy, foster a sense of community, and break down prejudice and biases.

According to Derald Wing Sue, a professor of psychology and education at Teachers College, Columbia University, a study in 2023 showed that 68 percent of Americans say microaggressions are a serious workplace problem. Sue said, "Microaggressions are the everyday slights, indignities, insults, put-downs, and invalidations that people of color experience in their day-to-day interactions with well-intentioned individuals who are unaware that they are engaging in an offensive or demeaning form of behavior." That includes microaggressions targeting sexual orientation, gender, and race. Another study, in the *Journal of Racial and Ethnic Health Disparities*, found that women and those with intersecting minority identities experienced higher levels of microaggressions than men and even more so than *white* men. Microaggressions can be unintentional or delivered as a compliment, but they are extremely harmful and can be devastating for mental health. By reading about others' experiences, watching a movie that depicts these struggles, or talking to victims of microaggressions can reduce their intensity and frequency.

SECOND

School provides a safe environment in which kids can learn, process, and gain experience before facing the real world.

Many children are entering high school with a number of negative life experiences. One in four girls and one in six boys have been sexually abused before the age of eighteen, according to the National Sexual Violence Resource Center. The American Society for the Positive Care of Children found that five children die every day from child abuse. According to the Centers for Disease Control and Prevention

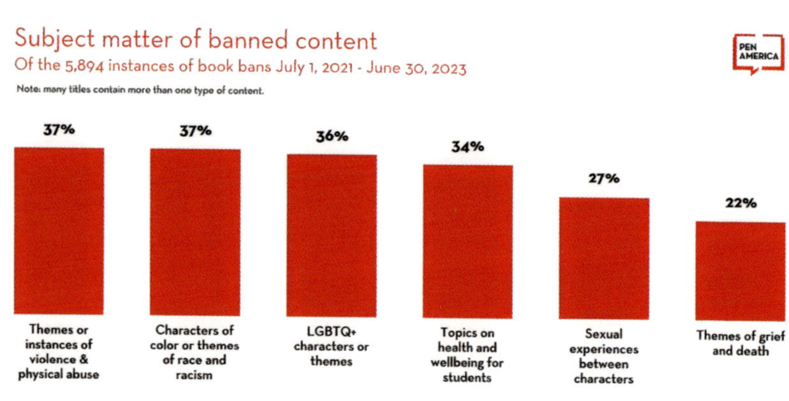

PEN America, a nonprofit organization that defends free expression in the United States, released this information that shows banned content by subject matter in a study from 2021–2023. Note how it disproportionately targets minorities.

(CDC), "More than half of U.S. high school students (55%) reported they experienced emotional abuse by a parent or other adult in the home." For many students, school is not only a place of education but also a place of safety. They can go there to have air-conditioning, heat, food, friends, supporters, resources, and security. It is a privilege to have a safe environment in which kids can learn about and process hard topics. Learning about these things prepares them for life outside of a school environment. For example, reading about sexual assault in a safe place with the freedom to ask questions of trusted adults can help someone feel prepared. Students can learn to be aware of unsafe environments and how to advocate for themselves if they encounter one.

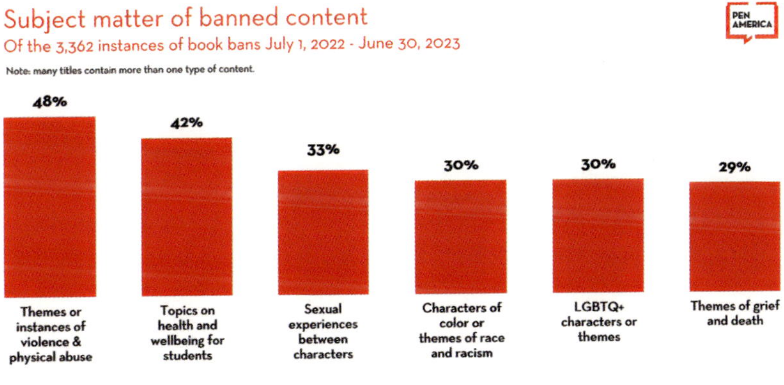

Another PEN study, this time of a single year (2022–2023), shows that LGBTQ+ and racial themes were still targeted, but there's a big jump in bans focusing on books discussing violence and well-being for students.

Books and discussions about hard subjects can help a student who felt alone and voiceless to feel seen, empowered, and strong enough to keep fighting.

The suggestion that schools should veer away from social-emotional learning is contradictory to what education entails. Social-emotional learning and "academic learning are inextricably linked and can't be separated," according to the Child Mind Institute. The five core components of social-emotional learning are self-awareness, social awareness, responsible decision-making, self-management, and relationship skills. It's a learning concept with many positive impacts. Students whose studies incorporated these five competencies performed better academically than those without. When students lack these skills in their education, "they often develop behavior problems that, in turn, can interfere with their functioning in school and their ability to learn."

Problem-solving, a skill that is formed and strengthened through the five competencies, can be found in nearly every subject. It is used regularly in mathematics and sewn into the English curriculum. Developing that skill early on and continuing to strengthen it provides students an advantage. Outside of the academic scope, social-emotional learning can prevent burnout among teachers and counselors, increase the likelihood of a person reaching important career-based milestones, reduce symptoms of depression and anxiety, aid in reducing bullying and aggression, and increase levels of "school functioning."

Education is not simply learning how to add. Education prepares you for the world it will one day release you into.

THIRD

Challenging books prepare students for college and beyond.

Included in social-emotional learning is exploring differing experiences and developing knowledge on how to handle them. Palomar College released an article that read, "When people read stories about other people's lives, it helps them develop the ability to understand the world through the lens of another person's perspective." It increases empathy and awareness. To defend banning books, many claimed that books like this carry topics that are too emotionally hard and difficult to digest. Similar to social-emotional learning, they claimed that those topics did not belong in schools. Various books on the list that were meant for a high school level detailed sexual discovery, racism's cruelty, experiences with abuse, the harms of microaggressions, spreading awareness, and combating mental health problems. I heard statements such as "The books will depress children" and "Students shouldn't be exposed to them."

What is forgotten and misunderstood for most book banners is that it's the librarian's job to decide where to place a certain book based on the demographic. No child would have an age-inappropriate book about hard topics such as sexual violence or racism in their library, just as very few nursery rhymes and picture books will be found in a high school. Allowing older students the *option* of reading about these difficult concepts, especially when many high schoolers have already been exposed to these topics in their lives, provides validation, awareness, increased empathy, and better preparation for the world around them. Reading and learning about difficult topics can prepare students for college and beyond.

As said previously, books can stand as "mirrors and windows." I was introduced to hard topics in college. I needed to have the capability to digest the material and have mature, respectful conversations in which a variety of opinions and experiences are shared. Because of the accessibility I had throughout my education at Central, I was prepared for that. I had learned how to have conversations that occasionally had uncomfortable content. I was able to comprehend material containing serious matters. I understood how to listen and provide a safe place for everyone in the room. I was prepared for the real world because I was introduced to social-emotional learning in school and because I had a safe place to confront difficult topics before I went to college. Not only did I read those materials, but I asked questions and took more advanced classes that dealt with these concepts. Luckily, I was provided the resources that educated me on such things as handling abuse, severe mental health problems, the Stonewall riots, microaggressions, and the dangers of discrimination. Without these opportunities, I would have been ill-prepared for college.

The real world is filled with emotionally taxing occurrences and constant social interactions. If we are not prepared for this in school, how would we be prepared? Students rely on school libraries to broaden their understanding, find representation, and receive accurate information, and book bans threaten this. Throwing a group of new adults into the world with no concept of how to handle emotional situations as well as social experiences that differ from the "norm" can result in conflict, polarization, and ignorance. But providing students with the resources to become accepting of all, to navigate various situations, and to gain experience in conversations with those different from themselves will create a group of adults that are ready to engage respectfully and better their surroundings. Ignorance can be just as dangerous as hate, but it can be prevented and fixed much more easily. These books and access to social and emotional education are the first steps to a more accepting and welcoming world.

By banning books, school boards are banning the voices of so many people. Every voice deserves to be heard, every story deserves to be recorded, and every person deserves to see themselves in a book. Banning books because they have the potential to trigger students is not right. Triggered responses are a personal thing, not the fault of others. The difference between a book and real life is this: You can walk away from a book. If a person begins reading a book that upsets them or brings on too many emotions from the past, they can choose to close the book and walk away. If a person is trying to learn about other experiences and gets too uncomfortable, they can close the book and walk away. The concern should not be about books. It should be about the real experiences these kids are forced to go through. It should be about finding ways to help students feel secure, validated, seen, and comforted.

WHAT TO SAY

When faced with the question of how social-emotional learning damages and triggers kids, respond this way:

- **Reading about their own experiences can help students feel validated and seen.**
- **School provides a safe environment in which kids can learn, process, and gain experience before facing the real world.**
- **Challenging books prepare students for college and beyond.**

CHAPTER 3

WILL DIVERSE BOOKS ENCOURAGE RACISM?

Renee Ellis, former director of communications and outreach and former president of PARU

As humans, we have found countless ways to identify ourselves and relate to one another. Having a strong sense of self is crucial because no one can define us; we must do that for ourselves. I'm a proud Black woman, a college student, a Central High School alum, a painter, a student activist, a music lover, and a Pinterest-obsessed artist. But, arguably more important, I am a hopeless, and sometimes naive, champion for humanity. I dream that the world will begin to fix the wrongs that have been plaguing our society for decades. The consequences of years and years of selfishness, greed, bad decisions, and cruelty continue to trickle down and affect my generation and the generations younger than me.

When I first heard of the book ban my school implemented, disbelief was the first emotion to settle in. Sadness, confusion, and anger soon followed. How could they do this? Why now? What is the point of this? When I was in middle school, I read *On the Come Up* by Angie Thomas. This book inspired me and other young Black girls. Yet this book, along with many others like it, was banned. The main character, Bri Jackson, has aspiring dreams of being an artist—more specifically a rapper. She is inspired by her father, and I am as well! The story follows Bri as she navigates growing into her true self, chases her dreams, fights for her identity as a Black woman, and overcomes the labels and pressures that society tries—but fails—to subject her to. That book meant the world to me because it was the first time I truly felt connected to a character. I finally found

***On the Come Up,* by Angie Thomas, was one of many titles by people of color on the banned books list in the Central York School District.**

a story that I could relate to my own life. *On the Come Up* helped me find my love for reading. Why was this book, my book, on the list? My mind raced to try to wrap itself around this unsettling reality. Books about diversity and inclusion are being banned, and it's not just a story in the news. It's a real-world problem that students and teachers are fighting all over. But why? Why are these resources being taken away? What is the reasoning behind these policies?

Angie Thomas, author of *On the Come Up*, speaks at Spelman College in September 2022.

Teachers, school administrators, and even government officials have had countless conversations about book bans. I've heard many different arguments in favor of book bans, but the one that I kept hearing was the argument that these books are unnecessary. I remember hearing people say that racism was no longer a problem. For example, while the book ban was being discussed, during the citizen's comments portions of several of the school board meetings, members of the community would share that they thought that there was no race problem in our district. Some would say that materials on diversity were unnecessary because they believed that racism was no longer a problem in America. This idea isn't just shared in York, Pennsylvania. On the news, in forums online, and even in political offices, this idea is being used to defend book banning. It stems from the argument that books about diversity and inclusion *create* racist divides rather than educating students about them. But the argument that racism is nonexistent is a slightly different statement.

It claims that the trials and tribulations that people of color in this country have gone through are also nonexistent. It claims that targeted policies, police brutality, and targeted hate crimes have nothing to do with race. It claims that every modern-day struggle people like me have faced is irrelevant and imaginary and that if racism is real, it is nothing but a problem people of color created for themselves.

I remember when my family and I lived in Idaho. I was around eleven years old. We visited a fellow church member (who was also Black), and we were watching a movie. The movie was an older film depicting the struggles and realities of life for African Americans after the abolition of slavery in America. On the screen, for the first time in my life, I saw in full color what happens to Black people when they come across the Ku Klux Klan. I was terrified, but I thought that it was just a show. Right? But the adults sat me down and explained to me that it might be a show, but it was based on true events. To my horror, we lived in an area where the Ku Klux Klan was active. I sat through an entire discussion on having to be careful not to run into a group like them. To this day, seeing the white gown and hood terrifies me. The argument that racism doesn't exist invalidates my experiences and implies that those conversations didn't happen or at least were of little value. That argument invalidates the reality that many people of color in this nation have had to and continue to live in fear of hate groups such as the Ku Klux Klan. People who deny racism also believe that books about diversity and inclusion "cause problems" and are meant to bring racism back into America. Hearing adults say that crushes me. But this idea contradicts itself! Well, almost. If given the proper context, it is easy to see a disconnect that allows me to build my counterarguments:

FIRST

Don't confuse race for racism.

American society has always had a hard time accepting its own history. There was a time when racism was the status quo. Your worth and value as a human being was determined by the color of your skin. There was a time where a Black person was considered a piece of property rather than a human being with rights. Activists throughout history have been killed for fighting against racism and for not wanting hatred to be the governing force in America. As America moved forward in time and ideologies, we started to hear "I don't see color." To me, when people say racism is nonexistent, I think of that statement. To not see color is to not see the whole of a person's identity. Race is defining. I know that might be an uncomfortable idea, but as a society, we need to understand that race is important, but not in the way America has made it important.

Colonizers, enslavers, and racists all created this idea that your race determines your worth and if you are not white, then you are property, garbage, disposable, good-for-nothing, and more. This has been seen throughout history—for example, the Supreme Court case *Dred Scott v. Sandford* (1857), the three-fifth compromise that enslaved people counted as three-fifth of a free person, Jim Crow laws, segregation, and the Supreme Court case of *Plessy v. Ferguson* that established the "separate but equal" doctrine. The list goes on. This is wrong. Very wrong. But that does not mean that race is wrong.

Your race is not a problem or something that should be changed. Everyone should be proud to be who they are. I am very proud to be Black. It is something that forever will be a part of how I identify myself. Every child should see themselves as beautiful no matter what race they are. A problem arises when we begin to hate one another because of our identities and when race becomes a measure of a person's worth and value. This is racism. No one deserves to live in a world where they are pressured to feel inferior based on the color of their skin. We need to celebrate one another for who we are. No longer should we turn away from the undeniable fact that humans come in all different shades. For some, trying to cancel race is an easy way to "solve" the hatred problem in our country. Just because someone says they don't see me as Black, doesn't mean

I am not Black. They cannot take my identity, culture, and experience away just because the conversation got uncomfortable. And it sure doesn't mean that I don't have to deal with the realities of being Black in America. The same goes for racism. Just because people claim that racism doesn't exist does not mean it has gone away. It just means they want to hide from the truth and ignore the work it takes to abolish the ideas of assimilation, color blindness, prejudice, and racism that bind this country.

Being able to see one another for who we truly are allows us to connect with one another. That means accepting other races, cultures, and identities while also respecting differences and uniqueness. Once America reaches that special place as a society, people can learn about different cultures, experience new places, and even hear others talk about their experiences and stories to inspire us in our own lives. America needs to see and accept race to understand that every human is deserving of equality. But this requires truth.

SECOND

Diversity resources help us to love ourselves and one another.

By learning about the lives of others and studying diversity, we grow to recognize our biases and have better compassion for ourselves and others, and we become more emotionally available to handle difficult conversations. According to the American Psychological Association, diversity education helps students uncover their *implicit* and *explicit* biases about other people. These can be difficult conversations to have, but they are necessary to learn how to have compassion and love for those that we might have nothing in common with. And uncovering our biases and learning to be inclusive of others will help us show better compassion to those whose lives and cultures we learn about. We can better understand human empathy by learning about the lives and struggles of other people. The American Psychological Association also says that it is hard for young learners to have difficult conversations. Talks about oppression, racism, and discrimination can inflict complicated and upsetting emotions. But feeling those emotions and working through them helps us to become stronger emotionally and mentally especially in communicating with others. Overall, when we learn about diversity, inclusion, and belonging, we can see how our lives fit into the tapestry of life. Through education, every student can further develop a sense of pride in who they are, their history, and where they come from.

Implicit bias refers to unconscious, automatic stereotypes or prejudices that influence a person's judgments and actions without their awareness.

Explicit bias refers to conscious, deliberate beliefs or attitudes that a person is aware of holding toward a particular group, often expressed openly.

Diversity and inclusion mean seeing one another for who we really are. Facing the truth. Each of us are different yet created to be earthmovers and world shakers. Every human is important. But we have not always treated one another well. Yes, people have been killed and mistreated because of their race. Still, people are being killed and mistreated for the same reason. The conversation is difficult. But if you do not want to call it racism, what is it then? It cannot be a coincidence because the same patterns of targeted killings and prejudice have been occurring in America for hundreds of years.

THIRD

Diversity resources teach us how to connect with one another and help to tear down racist and prejudiced beliefs.

Resources about diversity and inclusion are vital because they allow us to learn about the histories of people of color. For decades people of color in America have faced oppression, discrimination, and hate crimes. Defining the problem in our country as racism is the first step to solving it. We cannot make it go away by banning the resources that can help us to see how and why we need to abolish it! Children need to see and understand that race is not the problem. The problem is racism. These books help us to understand this idea and to see one another as beautiful. No longer does race need to be feared. Instead, every race deserves to be loved and supported. This is the message PARU worked to share.

As I said, I am a hopeless champion for society. I believe that we can and will do better once we make our voices heard. I was joined by friends and faculty who shared this dream, and we stood together in front of the school to make our voices heard. I remember sitting in our garage the day before the protest making posters advocating for students of color and equality. My sister and I brought those posters to school and stood in front of the school with a group of peers and faculty that listened to what we had to say, stood with us, and supported our efforts of activism. And the community soon followed.

During our fight against the book ban, I saw us students come together in a way I knew we could. Members of the community then came together to hold a book drive. PARU excitedly attended. Not only was the woman who organized the event a supporter of PARU, but also the idea of distributing the same books that were banned at our school into the community was enough for us to show up in full force. Right after school, I ran as fast as I could with my sister to experience this event. Despite arriving there minutes after it began, all the books were gone! Kids from all over the area came to receive materials that represented children who looked like them but also children who were different.

The organizers had everything covered. There were snacks, a place to take pictures, and tons of options for the kids. Thousands of books were given away that day, and I was able to speak to some of the parents and guardians who attended. They were so grateful for the opportunity and expressed to me that they felt that those diversity resources are so necessary for our community. With the ban in place, some parents were worried about their kids being able to access these resources but were glad to find that the community was coming together to ensure that no story was left untold. No child felt isolated. Kids of different races, backgrounds, and identities were present, and they all were able to find books that represented who they are.

I wished I had gotten my hands on at least one or two books, but I'm more grateful that the children were able to connect with one another through education and reading. The work has already begun. It is up to us to get down in the mud and join our friends, teachers, neighbors, and other fellow Americans in the fight for freedom. No longer are we hiding from our identities and from the reality of what America is. No matter what the argument is, book banning is a form of hiding. Books such as *I Am Malala* by Christina Lamb and Malala Yousafzai, *Long Way Down* by Jason Reynolds, *Hair Love* by Matthew A. Cherry, and so many others help to break the cycles of prejudice, bigotry, and hatred in this country.

Books that celebrate diversity do this:

- They help children to see that they are beautiful.
- They help children see that all other people are beautiful and that differences should be celebrated.
- They help to teach what racism is, that it is real, and why it is wrong.

These lessons are crucial for children to learn so that they grow into loving adults and strong leaders.

Choosing to ignore the problem and silencing the people who are the most affected by it is not the way out. When we ignore the problems being brought up, there tends to be that disconnect. Marginalized communities try to find love and pride in their race and identity, but it's seen as a threat by the rest of society. Differences among humans are seen as red flags, and people begin to think that race is wrong when racism is the beast needing to fall. Diversity is not an agenda target toward children to get them to believe in racism. It is a beautiful part of humanity. It is the hope that one day every human, along with their differences, will be accepted, represented, and seen as an equal.

I refuse to hide. I refuse to ignore the problem. Instead, I am standing tall, and I believe we are changing race relations not only for my generation but for generations to come.

WHAT TO SAY

When faced with the question of whether or not diverse books encourage racism, respond this way:

- **Don't confuse race for racism.**
- **Diversity resources help us to love ourselves and one another.**
- **Diversity resources teach us how to connect with one another and help to tear down racist and prejudiced beliefs.**

CHAPTER 4

DOES DISCUSSION OF DIVERSITY PROMOTE UNREST AND UNPATRIOTIC THOUGHTS?

Patricia A. Jackson, co-adviser of PARU

According to PEN (poets, playwrights, editors, essayists, and novelists) America, "A book ban occurs when an objection to the content of a specific book or type of book leads to that volume being withdrawn either fully or partially from availability, or when a blanket prohibition or absolute restriction is placed on a particular title within a school or a district."

As the district community became aware of the book ban, the argument over the resource list devolved into a war of semantics. The battle was led by two members of the board who insisted on referring to the mass ban as a temporary hold or freeze.

But a year after banning the materials, there was no movement or plan to vet, review, or discuss any of the titles. The truth became apparent: The school board had no intention of restoring the resources. "The fact that all the banned materials are by or about people of color is just a coincidence," the board president said to the press. The board also held up the approval of the social studies, math, and English curricula, newly written by teachers, and refused to vote on them until they could personally review the materials and suss out any potential influences from critical race theory.

By attempting to govern every detail of instruction in the classroom, the school board—which claimed to be working for the entire school community, including the 35 percent who were non-white—had become a specter of an antebellum past. It made me feel my Blackness was a blight to be stripped away and replaced by portraits of proper whiteness to ensure the comfort of white people in white spaces.

When a parent challenged the book *Push* by Sapphire, it was banned by an all-white panel appointed by the superintendent: a tech coach, the English Department head, the high school librarian, the high school principal, and the assistant superintendent. The novel—a harrowing story of a sexually abused, illiterate Black teenager who finds hope and self-worth through education and writing—was deemed pornographic, lacking any literary merit. With little to no knowledge of the Black experience, these so-called experts had no frame of reference to make any informed decisions. Strangely, I was not considered as an "expert" to be on that panel. I was the only Black teacher in the English Department, the only faculty member with a literary agent, and the only faculty member with an established list of publications. These credentials should count as expertise.

I remember the books I read as a child. The hot series of the time was V. C. Andrews's *Flowers in the Attic*, which the girls at my school read and passed around. After the death of her husband, the antagonist in the book locks up her four children in the attic so that she will not be disinherited by her millionaire father. The children, who are the product of an incestual heritage, are held captive for years. The eldest son and daughter come of age and go through puberty, where they begin experimenting sexually.

There was no public outcry, and I attended a private Catholic school, known to expel pregnant girls. Our parents were just happy to see us reading. I have always wondered: Was there no tumult among the general public because the characters acting badly in the book were white and upper class?

Ban or freeze, it no longer mattered. The words became synonymous and had an immediate chilling effect on teachers across the district. None of the resources on the list were part of the district curriculum, but many educators began removing any content from the approved curriculum that might be misconstrued as objectionable based on diversity.

This purge included excerpts from the celebrated enslaved narrative *Autobiography of Frederick Douglass*, the novel *Beasts of No Nation* by Uzodinma Iweala, and the poetry of Sojourner Truth, Nikki Giovanni, and Maya Angelou. A student pointed to a poster of Angelou that hung on a wall in my room and asked if I was afraid of being fired for having it. "Let them come," was my response, and she smiled with me in solidarity.

Afraid of losing their jobs, some district librarians quietly removed books that appeared on the resource list from the school libraries, categorizing them as "banned books" in the system. Even the preschool teacher removed any listed picture books to avoid scrutiny. The school board blamed PARU for causing a rift in the district, but they were the ones who had drawn a line through the community. Students, parents, and teachers found themselves forced to choose a side.

In the wake of the ban, PARU was making ripples, not only in the local community but across the nation and even internationally! Our fight for diversity was being talked about in lofty places, garnering praise from best-selling authors, politicians, and historic notables. Words of encouragement came from legislators such as Senator Bob Casey (D-PA), Representative Jamie Raskin (D-MD), and Pennsylvania State Representative Malcolm Kenyatta. Casey personally reached out to talk with the executive board of PARU, as did then–Pennsylvania Attorney General Josh Shapiro. Tom Wolf, the then governor of Pennsylvania, invited PARU to the state capitol to support legislation to fight book bans.

Thanks to Charlyn Henderson of Columbia University, my "coconspirator" Ben Hodge and I were treated to a phone call from Carolyn Maull and praised for the work of the club. Maull was fifteen in 1963 when she answered the phone and received a bomb threat minutes before an explosive device went off in the Sixteenth Street Baptist Church in Alabama. This terrorist attack by a white supremacist killed four little girls. Our work even caught the eyes

Members of the second generation of PARU receive the Youth Influencer Award from the King Center in January 2021. ***Left to right*****: Ben Hodge, Patty Jackson, Christina Ellis, Dr. Bernice King, Edha Gupta, Olivia Pituch, and Renee Ellis.**

of Jane Elliott, whose controversial work to fight racism is still raising eyebrows across the nation.

PARU won awards. Though the school board refused to acknowledge PARU's growing list of merits and achievements, our advocacy was recognized by the York County Economics Alliance; the Martin Memorial Library, which commissioned an art installation by Ophelia Chambliss to be hung in the teen section; and Red Wine and Blue, which helped the executive officers have the opportunity to testify before the US Congress. Two members of the executive board of PARU were invited to testify in person as to the harm being done by book bans in our district and our community. Later that year, PARU would be recognized by the King Center CEO, Bernice King, the youngest daughter of Martin Luther King Jr. We attended a star-studded event in Atlanta, Georgia, to be honored by the Beloved Community as Teen Influencers.

Despite the accolades, many community members remained on the fence about the book ban and the repercussions of the media attention, which many considered to be negative. There were reports that major businesses were allegedly avoiding Central York because of the scrutiny and were having trouble relocating staff who did not want their children attending the schools. Some of these neutral people were confused by the bombardment of misinformation fed to them by the board, and others could not believe a book ban was happening in the twenty-first century. Like the school board, most had not read any of the books. Others only read cherry-picked excerpts without the benefit of context or form. When the district's stakeholders, parents, taxpayers, and other concerned citizens argued the pros and cons of the ban, I jumped at the opportunity to broaden their understanding about the dog whistles being used against them.

FIRST

Book bans are not a movement to protect children. They are politically motivated attempts to rewrite history. Erasing the life experiences of Black people during slavery, Jewish people during the Holocaust, or Native Americans during the westward expansion of America offers a false narrative of what really happened. It is a way for white people who are uncomfortable with the past to bury the misdeeds of their forefathers, our forefathers, and maintain a role of dominance over people of color.

Diversity unites us through shared stories that uplift the life experiences of *all* people, circumventing the notion that one race is superior to another. The idea that teachers or the teaching of diverse history will make white kids feel guilty is a ploy to trigger white parents. This is a textbook attempt to defend *white fragility*. I don't see the same vigor being used to advocate for mental health services for students or to deal with the problem of drugs and alcohol in our schools. These are real issues that cause real harm among our youth.

***White fragility* is a term coined by sociologist Robin DiAngelo that refers to the discomfort white people may feel when confronted with racism.**

Consider the story of six-year-old Ruby Bridges. In 1954 the Supreme Court shot down the *Plessy v. Ferguson* case, which had allowed for the segregation of schools. In 1960 Ruby became the first Black student to enter William Frantz Elementary School in New Orleans, Louisiana. Out of concern for her safety, she was escorted by federal marshals while a mob of white people stood outside the school to threaten her.

History has the receipts: the names and pictures of the men and women who shouted and cursed at her. The grandchildren and great-grandchildren of these instigators are seeing those receipts printed in history books and questioning why. Rather than offering a teachable explanation for their racist behavior, some people are leading the charge to ban books and bury or rewrite the past.

In my American literature class, I use the film *4 Little*

Girls by Spike Lee as a segue into the Civil Rights Movement. The film documents the racial tensions that led to the 1963 bombing of the Sixteenth Street Baptist Church in Birmingham, Alabama, which galvanized the movement to gain equal rights for Black people in this country.

A white student, who had been expelled from the local vocational school for shouting "white power" at Black students, returned to our district, and by some stroke of luck, he was placed in my English class. I welcomed him, believing that, with the right tools and support, he could grow beyond his earlier harmful behavior.

After watching *4 Little Girls*, he came up to my desk, looking down at his belt buckle, a replica of the Confederate flag. He said, "I can never see this flag the same way again, Ms. Jackson." He never wore it again.

This is an example of critical thinking and reflection, not guilt or shame. There was no fragility here. This was a child who had his eyes opened to what happened in a terrible moment in American history, and he made a conscious choice not to promote hatred. To this day, this young man keeps in touch with me and refers to me as "Mom."

SECOND

Teachers are not indoctrinating students with unpatriotic ideals.

An African proverb says: "The ruin of a nation begins in its homes." This is true. Real indoctrination does begin at home, not in the classroom.

The Bible says, "Love your neighbor as yourself."

People who are in favor of book bans often give the Bible the same cherry-picking once-over they do with objectionable books, choosing the verse to justify their actions, while ignoring any counterarguments printed in the Word of God.

Children aren't born hating someone because of the color of their skin, sexual orientation, or religion. Children are uniquely curious and forgiving when raised to respect all people based on their character, as the Reverend Martin Luther King Jr. surmised. But under the guise of parental concern and Christian right, members of groups like Moms for Liberty insist that "not every human is worthy of my child's empathy." This quote is taken from the legal documents of a lawsuit in the West Shore School District in Pennsylvania. Supported by the hate group, right-wing parents are attempting to stop the adoption of curriculum that would teach empathy and understanding.

Bigotry is modeled behavior. But the cost is evident when children brought up around bigotry are among their peers at school. Feeling no need to assert dominance, white children wrestle with the lessons being taught at home, which conflict with sharing a safe place in school where all are welcomed, regardless of race, creed, or sexual orientation.

A student was giving feedback on a presentation by a transmasculine student and accidentally misgendered them. I interceded to correct him because I knew it was important to this student to be recognized as male with he/him pronouns.

The young commentator apologized to his classmate, corrected the pronoun, and proceeded with his feedback. It's that simple! Courtesy costs nothing. Respect is everything!

Diverse books share the trials, tribulations, and victories of marginalized people, allowing children to empathize and reflect on the similarities and differences of their own life experiences. But some people, including anti-Black extremists, have mischaracterized all things related to diversity, equity, and inclusion as threats to non-marginalized individuals or communities. This is untrue and unfounded.

Banning or freezing these materials says to children who have experienced similar traumas that something is inherently wrong with them, and that *they*, like the books, need to be removed or erased.

The voters spoke at the polls to vote out some of the more radical members of the board. But the ousted members pressured the remaining directors to continue the attack on books, parental rights, and student choice.

A defeated opponent is a wiser opponent, learning from their past mistakes. So rather than a broad ban on books, the board attacked a smaller, select number of books under the guise of parental concern. One of those books was *Push* by Sapphire. Using an administrative regulation that was meant for books taught in the curriculum, the school board tried to apply the rule to books in the library.

The complainant was a parent who had failed to get elected to the board. Her identity was initially hidden from the public to shield her from pushback. No one knew about her or the removal of the book until right-wing supporters began congratulating themselves on social media. Once it was made known, PARU jumped into action to demand a change to the policy, which had no bearing on library books, and to force the district to return the books to the stacks.

When Sapphire became aware of the ban, she wrote an eloquent statement to the school board, which I read at one of the meetings. One of the comments Sapphire wrote seemed to be a premonition of what York County and across the country would come to be: "When we ban books like *Push*, we are in danger of falling into the sink-holes of hate and prejudice and ignorance, and of losing what little love we have left for each other."

WHAT TO SAY

When faced with the question of whether or not discussion of diversity promotes unrest and unpatriotic thoughts, respond this way:

- **Book bans are not a movement to protect children. They are politically motivated attempts to rewrite history.**
- **Children aren't born hating someone because of the color of their skin, sexual orientation, or religion.**

CHAPTER 5

DOES TEACHING BLACK HISTORY ENCOURAGE WHITE KIDS TO HATE AMERICA OR THEMSELVES?

Ben Hodge, founder and co-adviser of PARU

I am a theater and English teacher at Central York High School. I am also the artistic director for Central York Performing Arts. I've been fortunate enough to spend all twenty-three years of my career as an educator in one district. This has allowed me to really understand the ins and outs of our school community. I love our community, the programs we offer, my amazing colleagues, and my talented students.

One of the most beneficial programs that I have been involved in is Central York School District's Diversity Committee. I have worked on this committee since 2007 and have always considered myself a staunch advocate of diversity and inclusion initiatives. Central York High School was one of the first local York schools to add a social worker and diversity specialist, and I remember connecting with them as soon as they were announced. Some of our tasks through the years included classroom management discussions; one-on-one mediations with staff and students; conflict resolution; staff trainings on identity, race and culture; and planning and leading diversity celebrations. This was the first time in my career where I was working closely with people of color, and these years were the most formative and rewarding years of my career. I learned key foundational skills that helped me to be a better teacher to *all* of my students, and I gained a new thirst for Black history and things that I wasn't taught in my own schooling as a kid.

During the COVID-19 pandemic and after the murder of George Floyd, I found myself even more hungry for knowledge about Black history and the issues of white supremacy. I have always loved American history, so it was natural for me to dig into an aspect of the past that I didn't know much about. One of the books that I picked up during this personal reflection was *Me and White Supremacy* by Layla Saad. This book challenged my views on my concept of racism and the effects it has on society.

Me and White Supremacy was informative about terms and definitions for the latest racial reckoning, but it also challenged me to move past being an ally in identity only and become an ally in practice. Until then, most of my love of history had stayed within the walls of my classroom, and it did not affect my life outside of the classroom. One of the quotes that resonated with me the most from the book was

"Allyship is not an identity but a practice . . . do not proclaim to be an ally but seek to practice allyship consistently."

After reading this book and observing all that was going on in the country at that time, I knew I needed to take a bigger action. I formed PARU as a response to that challenge from Saad's book. At its inception, PARU was designed to replicate the conversations that were organically occurring in my theater classes surrounding race, identity, culture, and artistic expression. The club was for anyone who was interested in meeting for honest discussions about these topics in a safe and courageous space. I decided early on that I wanted the word *Union* to be in the name of the group because I knew and had experienced the power of a unified group: People from all backgrounds and cultures coming together to learn together can be a powerful and transformational experience. Early on in the creation of PARU, I reached out to my good friend and colleague in the English Department, Patty Jackson, who joined on as co-adviser to the club.

After forming PARU, we invited students to meet via Zoom. Those early days were so exciting—it was a beautiful thing to watch the club grow and hear the conversations that the students initiated. At its inception in June 2020, our meetings once a week included about six to eight students. Because of the pandemic, these meetings were held virtually and primarily occurred after school. That was a feat in itself . . . to get students to show up to another Zoom call after they sat in video conference classrooms for the whole day.

After we were able to return to school, PARU started to meet in person during our club time from 2:00 to 2:45 p.m. At the beginning, these meetings consisted of goal planning, club leadership structure, and education. The students brainstormed and discussed issues that they were dealing with or wanted to learn about. They mentioned how they didn't know much about certain individuals from Black history, so we researched some of those people and began to discover as much as we could about them. The group also wanted to include an activism goal in the club vision. For the first several months, the education and conversation continued until we were thrown into what we called "activism mode." Little did I know that the creation of this activism goal would be one of the key elements of PARU's success.

Our school board meetings at this time were being held remotely, and I remember first tuning in to hear what they were saying about masking and school closures. What I heard instead was much worse. Around this time, Patty and I joined the aforementioned group of teachers who were gathering materials and resources related to diversity, equity, inclusion, and representation to make sure that our school community was better prepared to handle conversations about race. Somewhere in those planning meetings, some of the board members started to join the meetings and took offense to what was being discussed. The school board was caught up in the backlash against the racial reckoning that was occurring after Floyd's murder and began to

A school board member shields her face from people participating in a protest outside the Central York School District Educational Service Center on September 21, 2020.

speak about banning materials and diversity trainings. Around this time, national arguments had broken out about critical race theory. Seemingly without a strong grounding on what it was, the school board echoed these arguments, claiming that the district was somehow trying to use Floyd's death as a way to insert diversity, equity, and inclusion initiatives into the schools without any oversight.

PARU was one of the first groups to hear these comments and helped to share them with other teachers, students, and families within the district. I remember sitting in on these board meetings and hearing these arguments and claims that diversity was hurting our school, and I felt confused, angry, and frustrated. Central had a tradition of diversity, equity, and inclusion initiatives since 2007, and it was not something that anyone was trying to "sneak in." Over and over again, I heard school board members and citizens repeat this same argument: Learning about Black history and having conversations about race teaches kids to hate America or hate themselves.

I think this argument was used to stall the group's work of pulling together diversity resources and to cast doubt and cause confusion about its intentions. We were told to remove resources from our classrooms that highlighted stories written by authors of color and authors from marginalized backgrounds. The board pushed out a local diversity speaker who was slated to lead our professional development day at the start of the 2020 school year. Suddenly, these board members were asking about intentions. We were told to stop making lists of books that could help students discuss race, identity, and culture and to eliminate these resources before they were discussed or read. The board claimed they were dangerous and unfit for anyone to read. In their words, they were dangerous because they were teaching young people to hate America, not respect the police and adopt "Marxist" or "anti-American" beliefs. Instead of recognizing the importance of educating ourselves on these topics, they chose to sow fear and misinformation about the validity of these efforts.

Then PARU decided to get more active in speaking out against these actions and this rhetoric. I started with organizing the first of three community protests that were held outside of the Education Service Center, where the board meetings were held remotely. At this point, our club of about six to eight students doubled in size to about fifteen to twenty active members. I asked students from PARU to speak and share their feelings about these claims. Other local organizations, community members, parents or guardians, and teachers joined in as well, so we had over 250 people gathered together with signs that shared our counterpoints: *Diversity Is Our Strength, This Is Not the Central I Know, Education Is Not Indoctrination, We Are Stronger Together*, and more. At these first protests, I was reminded of the power and joy within our Central York family. There was music, laughter, camaraderie, support, and passion for what was right. It made me realize that PARU was not alone and that people supported our efforts to stand up against the board.

The national media had already been covering the racial reckoning after Floyd's murder, so when the local news learned about the community protest through social media, they began to report regularly about the story. PARU were interviewed about the issue, and we shared some of these counterarguments with the public. During these interviews and speeches, I shared three counterarguments when asked about when people say, "We should remove books by Black authors because learning about Black history makes students hate America and hate themselves."

FIRST

Black history is American history.

As an avid history lover, I didn't know much about Black history because it hadn't been adequately taught or supported in my education. I grew up in predominantly white spaces and only learned about slavery, the Civil War, and a brief section on the Civil Rights Movement. Looking at our textbooks and curricula today, I think this is still true. There was little to nothing about Crispus Attucks, Marcus Garvey, Reconstruction, *Black codes*, *Jim Crow*, Ida B. Wells, Thurgood Marshall, Angela Davis, or other Black history heroes and trailblazers.

Black codes: Laws passed in Southern states after the Civil War to limit the rights of formerly enslaved people

Jim Crow: A system of racial segregation laws that enforced racial apartheid in the Southern United States from the 1880s to the 1960s

After making up for lost time reading as much Black history as I could (I still am!), I argued that learning about Black history doesn't make me hate America. It actually makes me believe in it more. I learned to believe in America even more after I read about Harriet Tubman, Bayard Rustin, Fannie Lou Hamer, Shirley Chisholm, Misty Copeland, and others who overcame extremely difficult situations and extreme racism to still fight for and believe in freedom, justice, and liberty for all.

Learning more about Black history helped me develop an honest and realistic view of America, rather than the myth of American exceptionalism that I grew up on. America is a great nation. But it is not without its faults and shortcomings. It is imperative for us as people to seek the truth in all things, and learning more about our country, both the good and the bad, helps me understand the role I can play as a member of this society. It helps me

TRAILBLAZERS IN BLACK HISTORY

- **Crispus Attucks: An American sailor of African and Native American descent who is commonly referred to as the first person killed in the Boston Massacre and also the first American killed in the American Revolution**
- **Marcus Garvey: A Jamaican political activist who founded the Universal Negro Improvement Association and African Communities League**
- **Ida B. Wells: A Black American investigative journalist, sociologist, educator, and early leader in the Civil Rights Movement**
- **Thurgood Marshall: The United States Supreme Court's first African American justice**
- **Angela Davis: A Black American feminist political activist, philosopher, academic, and author**

work toward creating a more perfect union. It helps me be a better neighbor because I have learned things that are outside of my lived experience. I think the people arguing that Black history is teaching people to hate America are missing the value of respecting and honoring the truth vs. a myth and misinterpreting the criticism of calls for progress and growth as an attack on the foundation of America.

Criticism and feedback are crucial for any society or person. Sometimes it is imperative for me to hear about something that I am doing wrong so that I can change it.

So it is with a country. The literary critic, author, and activist James Baldwin once said, "I love America more than any other country in the world and, exactly for this reason, I insist on the right to criticize her perpetually." Criticism does not mean there is an absence of love and respect. On the contrary, criticism when done respectfully and honestly can come from a place of great love and admiration.

When I learn about Black history, I learn things that frustrate, scare, and disgust me. But there are also things that are inspiring about it. It gives me hope that this country one day can become what it set out to be: a place where all people have life, liberty, and the pursuit of happiness. When I learn about Black history, my love of America grows and my commitment to stand and speak up for what is right blossoms. I want to do what Martin Luther King Jr. said: "to make America what it ought to be. We have an opportunity to make America a better nation." We can only do this if we accept the truths of the past and work to fix them in the future.

SECOND

It's not about shame and guilt. It is about learning and accepting the truth.

There is a real fear among those who are calling for the removal of Black history resources that somehow learning the truth about our history will make white people hate themselves. I think this is a ridiculous argument for many reasons. I countered this argument saying that it is emotion that is both misinterpreted and misplaced. I think the anger and frustration that white people feel when learning about things like *Tuskegee*, Black codes, and lynchings is appropriate and justified. There is a sense of shame that I feel as a white person when reading about these things. It is vile and indescribable to think how one race, or any group of people, could do these things to another simply based on the amount of melanin in their skin. But as a white male, I don't read about the Tulsa race massacre and think, *I hate myself because my race did that.* I ask things like "How could this have happened?" And the answer is pretty clear: There was or is a system of white supremacy in place to perpetuate and support these actions. How else could a country time after time turn its eyes from the atrocities it was dishing out to a significant portion of its population?

Tuskegee: Starting in 1932 and lasting until 1972, the U.S. Public Health Service (USPHS) ran a study in Tuskegee, Alabama. They recruited hundreds of African American men, many of them poor and uneducated, and told them they were being treated for "bad blood," a general term for various illnesses. But here's the horrifying truth: These men had syphilis, a sexually transmitted infection, and the doctors never gave them the actual treatment that could have cured them.

Feeling a sense of shame and guilt isn't always just negative emotions. I think the people making this argument misinterpret these emotions and make them only a bad thing. Shame and guilt also lead to growth and forgiveness. Perhaps that is it: that many who make this argument feel that they will not be forgiven or that they have to live in constant shame for the actions of the past. Learning about white supremacy and the truth about Black history in our country is not about wallowing in that shame or guilt. It is about growth, understanding, and doing something about it. Saad said it this way: "The purpose of this work is not for you to end up living in shame. The purpose is to get you to see the truth so that you can do something about it."

Learn the truth. Be hurt and inspired by it. I must resist the urge to wallow in that shame or joy. I must always strive to do what I can to make this world a better place.

THIRD

Learning about Black history doesn't make one hate being white. It helps one to be a better person.

Learning about Black history reminds me of a choice that I have: What kind of person will I be? Will I be one who amplifies, supports, and listens to my Black and brown brothers and sisters, or will I be one who fears those who don't look or think like me? Will I be one who will learn to spend any privilege that I have to help the marginalized and less fortunate not only survive but thrive? Learning about Black history makes me realize that much work still needs to be done toward progress and freedom. It teaches me that there is still so much that I do not know about our history. I must remain hungry for that knowledge because knowledge is power.

The truth is so powerful that it makes sense in some respects to keep the truth about our history secret and restricted. For some people, once you learn about how things operate and who is pulling the strings, you can't help but do something about it. Look at how people have co-opted the word *woke* to mean something that is anti-white. This word was originally coined by Black progressives in the 1900s. To be "woke" means that someone is informed, educated, and conscious of social injustice and racial inequality. That's it. It never meant "anti-white" or "anti-American." Yet that is what many perceive it as.

Being woke has nothing to do with being anti-white. It doesn't make white people hate themselves. If anything, it provides a path to a better understanding of self and others. It teaches me to be mindful about my relationships with others and how easily I can fall into traps of white saviorism or white privilege. White saviorism is when any white person tries to "help" people of color in a way that seems to put themselves in the spotlight and ignores the actual needs and abilities of the people they're trying to help. I know that I am not here to save anyone who doesn't look like me. White privilege is the set of advantages that white people have in society simply because they are white. It doesn't mean that white people don't struggle or that they haven't worked hard, but it does mean recognizing that many white folks don't face the same kinds of obstacles and discrimination that people of color do. Being "woke" doesn't make me feel bad as a white person; it just reminds me that I need to stand for justice and equality and use any privilege that I have to help marginalized groups where I can.

Learning about Black history and the truth about white supremacy in this country doesn't make me hate America or myself for being white. It answers key questions such as "How could racial apartheid (a system of fierce, strict and coordinated segregation and discrimination based on race) in a 'free' country happen?" or "How did groups like the Ku Klux Klan even exist and operate?" It helps me to be a better person. It helps me to be more empathetic and understanding. I think knowing the full truth makes me a better American as well because it opens me up to fighting for freedom for *all* people, not just those who look like me.

Saad challenged me in 2020 to learn to be a good ancestor . . . someone who leaves this world better for those who will come in the future: "I want to speak to the good ancestor who lies within you, the person inside you who came to this book with questions about dismantling white supremacy and who leaves this book knowing that you are a part of the problem and that you are simultaneously also a part of the answer. There is great power and responsibility in that knowledge. But knowledge without action is meaningless."

I hope you all hear that call to be a good ancestor. Learning the truth about what happened in our country is not about shame. It's about the fight for freedom and the power of a people to overcome extreme odds. Isn't that what some of us are taught about the greatness of America? People can come here to create a new and more prosperous life from little to nothing. That's what all kinds of history, including Black history, have shown me. It has taught me about determination, resiliency, grit, and hope through the darkest and vilest of circumstances. That's what I want to lean into. Hope. Perseverance. Determination. Not shame. The more I live in shame and ignorance to the truth, the less action I take to make this world a better place. With all that I have learned, I cannot go back to staying silent about the things that really matter. I hope it will be the same with you.

WHAT TO SAY

When faced with the question of whether or not teaching Black history encourages white kids to hate America or themselves, respond this way:

- **Black history is American history.**
- **It's not about shame and guilt. It is about learning and accepting the truth.**
- **Learning about Black history doesn't make one hate being white. It helps one to be a better person.**

CHAPTER 6

DO DIVERSITY RESOURCES GLORIFY TRAUMATIC EXPERIENCES?

Renee Ellis, former director of communications and outreach and former president of PARU

I can imagine that being a parent and having to prepare your kids for any and every negative experience they might face is an incredibly difficult job. My own parents have worked so hard to ensure that my sister and I would be prepared for whatever life could throw at us. One of the harshest realities to accept is that everyone will face pain at some point in their lives—including your children. I believe we would all wish, to some extent, to have an easy and happy life, but negative experiences are part of being a human being.

The saying goes, no pressure, no diamonds. But some parents worry about their kids knowing about the traumas of this world. Some parents don't want their kids to be exposed to different life stories, especially if they haven't experienced it themselves. This is another area where book bans come into play. Censorship has been used many times to keep diverse experiences and stories at bay.

Every parent has their way of raising their children. There is no one-size-fits-all for parenting. One person's wishes for their child doesn't reflect every parent's wishes for their own children. Also, every child is different. Our parents instilled a strong sense of faith in my sister and me. My faith has helped me through the traumatic experiences I faced in my life. My parents also protected me from inappropriate content, overly sexual materials, and the dangers of the real world. But they never had my sister or me shun the stories of others. Every human being has a story. Yes, some are more brutal than others and are not for younger audiences, but that doesn't mean they should be silenced. Relatability helps us cope through our trials and tribulations. How do the children who are still struggling through traumatic experiences find help without resources?

Some kids don't have parental or adult figures in their lives who assist them through the challenges of life. It's easy to forget that diversity is all encompassing. Some children live in abusive homes, don't have food to eat when they get home, live in dangerous neighborhoods, or face other challenges. According to the Greater Good Science Center at the University of California, Berkeley, diversity resources are crucial because schools can provide significant help for whatever students may be going through in their personal lives.

When my school banned their diversity resource list in 2020, one of the arguments used to defend the decision was that diversity resources glorify traumatic experiences. Not one of the faculty members that I knew held this belief, but plenty of parents did. They could not relate to some of the truth written on the pages so they became defensive. Part of the work PARU had to do was educate others on the reasons why diversity resources are needed. We built our counterarguments, explaining that diversity resources do not glorify trauma but, instead, are necessary for learning.

FIRST

Without diversity resources, teachers are helpless.

Teachers have become more than just educators. Teachers, principals, and school administrators are therapists, social workers, parents and, for some kids, their first line of defense. Schools no longer have the luxury of just being places of learning. Some schools have become the only safe havens for children who have been traumatized, and educators are having to adapt to being more than what is listed on their degree.

Teachers need resources that talk about the real struggles many kids face to help them not only be successful teachers but also to fulfill the roles that have been placed upon them. Diversity resources help bridge the gap. They help teach educators about the lives of their students. How can an educator be impactful in a situation or environment they know nothing about? How will educators be able to connect to their students?

I once had a teacher ask me if it was okay to compliment a Black girl's hair. The way the teacher approached me, I thought his question would be controversial, but he genuinely wanted to know if he could compliment her hair. He wasn't sure if it would be received as a compliment or if it would be received as a sly insult or microaggression. Because race relations are in a tough place, our society has been trained to avoid race conversations. Some teachers don't know how to proceed. Diversity resources teach us how to operate in inclusive environments. Books such as *Hair Love* by Matthew A. Cherry, *One Crazy Summer* by Rita Williams-Garcia, and *Piecing Me Together* by Renee Watson shed light on Black culture, Black womanhood, and some Black people's views about their hair. Those books

The picture book, *Hair Love*, by Matthew Cherry (*left*) was challenged in the Central York School District, one of many challenged books by people of color.

would've helped anyone to approach the topic of hair. If some books explore unfortunate situations surrounding microaggressions, cultural appropriation, or offensive language, they don't glorify those experiences. Instead, they teach readers how to navigate the situations. Unfortunately, the diversity resources that help bridge the gap between faculty and students have come under fire.

SECOND

Sharing the realities that marginalized communities go through helps build stronger communities.

The Hate U Give by Angie Thomas is one of my favorite books. (I am a huge Angie Thomas and Jason Reynolds fan!) It was one of the books that I read in middle school that changed how I viewed reading for the rest of my life. The main character, Starr, has to deal with many challenges in her life. She has to deal with not fitting into the majority-Black community she was raised in, while also not fitting into the majority-white school she attends—an experience I relate to. But one of the biggest challenges she has to face is watching her close friend Khalil be murdered by the police.

Starr has to cope with that traumatic experience and the memories of other traumatic experiences flooding her mind as she sees Khalil's lifeless body in front of her. Worse yet, his killer is a police officer, which brings up police brutality—not foreign to many Black households in America.

The book ends with conflict resolution, and the reader sees Starr transform and heal from the hardship she has faced. But just as importantly, the reader reads about her pain. That might seem like something any person would want to avoid, but we can't keep running from the real problems that people face in life. Of course, books need to be age appropriate for readers, and it is important to be conscious of the materials being given to children and students. But as a society, silencing and ignoring real-world issues does not make them go away and neither does it take away the hurt that so many people have faced. Care, love, compassion, hope—these things are needed to heal a broken society, but the first step is admitting it is broken. Diversity resources open our eyes to real problems and teach us how to show care, love, compassion, and hope, even in situations we haven't experienced ourselves.

For me, personally, it means a lot that Starr is so much like me. I have not seen anyone murdered, but I have gone through my own set of challenges. Reading how Starr dealt with her pain helped me to handle my own issues. It gave me a different perspective to consider. More importantly, it gave me a point of reference. I can go back and point out experiences that Starr went through that I have gone through as well. I can use those moments to help me in my personal life but also to connect with other people. A teacher could read a passage that I relate to and could better understand where I am coming from. That teacher could also read around that passage to gain context, knowledge, and information on how to address the situation if needed. That is what diversity resources do. They provide information on other people's lives and experiences without which we might not have been able to relate.

THIRD

As uncomfortable as it is, we need to learn about the hard stuff so that we can be better and raise the next generation to be better.

Teachers need these resources as much as the students do. Some members of the Central York community argue that these resources glorify tragic situations, but learning about other experiences is not glorifying trauma, it's relating to being human. Just because we haven't experienced what someone has gone through, that does not mean we can't learn from it. As a society, we should want to understand the problems that others face. We could learn how to better situations instead of worsening them. Although we all go through some sort of pain, it might not all be the same, but pain is still pain.

The next generation of students coming into the classrooms are bringing their own set of struggles but also their own set of bad habits. Hatred, bigotry, and intolerance are taught, but so are acceptance, kindness, and inclusion. We need a practice of reaching out and connecting to other people ingrained in us to develop better habits.

By the time I turned eighteen, I had lived in five different states and over fifteen different houses. I met people from all different walks of life and had to learn how to be accepting of all people, no matter if we shared similar stories. Not every child has that privilege. Books about different lives and cultures allow readers to enter into a world foreign to them.

Seeing things that we are not used to and opening up to new experiences can be scary. But to move forward as a society, we need to stop hiding. Communities need to stop banning resources. We need to see different perspectives and value one another. People become better when they stop fighting one another and instead work to understand one another.

It is unfair to expect teachers to know how to deal with any and every situation thrown at them without resources to assist them. And it is unfair to subject people to suffering in silence. These materials are needed, and they help us grow into better people. While some stories might be hard to read, their impact is monumental. A story is inside each of us that has the ability to shape who we are as a person.

It is also important to consider that some people can handle certain things more easily than others, but that does not discredit or erase that the person is struggling. What might be viewed as horribly grotesque and traumatic for some might not be as extreme for others. There is a beauty in that as well. Some people can handle certain situations in ways that allow them to more readily support others. We can help one another break cycles of generational pain and systematic corruption. But to help, we must first understand. We can only do better if we know better. And once we know better, we can teach the younger generations to be better as well.

WHAT TO SAY

When faced with the question of whether or not diversity resources glorify traumatic experiences, respond this way:

- **Without diversity resources, teachers are helpless.**
- **Sharing the realities that marginalized communities go through helps build stronger communities.**
- **We need to learn about the hard stuff so that we can be better and raise the next generation to be better.**

CHAPTER 7

SHOULD EDUCATION STICK TO CORE SUBJECTS?

Christina Ellis, vice president of PARU, 2021–2022

I remember tension in the air during social studies units about slavery and the Civil Rights Movement. I was often the only Black kid in the class. The students in my class who stared at me had angry looks within their eyes or looked worried or just had a blank stare. For me, an elementary school kid, this was uncomfortable. During my K–12 schooling, I became used to that feeling. Kids and even staff at school would run their hands through my hair without permission and proceed to ask whether my hair was natural. In middle school, I begged my parents to let me straighten my hair to "fit in" with my classmates. I had grown tired of classmates and staff touching my hair. At times, I wanted nothing more than to blend in. I battled with my identity as a Black girl in America, how my natural hair looked, and the history of African Americans in America. I was not ashamed of who my people are, but I was irritated by being picked on. Fast-forward to the start of PARU and I explored my identity as an African American, including my relationship with my hair. PARU was built to advocate for students of all backgrounds. Being a leader in 2021–2022 allowed me to share my story to help other students like me.

PARU raised awareness of the book ban in the Central York School District in York. The books banned were about diversity and inclusion. An argument made in favor of the book ban was that education shouldn't include social-emotional learning but should stick to core subjects. Here are my rebuttals against that.

FIRST

Students need to learn how to interact with others who are different from them.

A school is also a place for students to learn how to be social and communicate effectively.

Students learning how to interact with others who are different from them is crucial. Being different from someone else is not bad, it's what makes the world we live in unique. Students should be able to be in a school with any identities they have and be able to learn and socialize without discrimination from students and staff. A school is where students initially learn to socialize and be among those outside of their household. Why can't schools be a place for students to learn to be respectful of people who are not identical to them? Schools can be where they learn and grow and see that students of all different backgrounds are smart and capable.

What happens when students go on to college, get a job, and move out of the school and home they know? Students will eventually turn the tassels on their graduation cap over and become young adults. They will have to enter society and experience a world full of mysteries. Students will not be kids forever. They will soon be in government, hospitals, and corporate offices. We can't raise kids to think their way of life is the only way to live. Students need to be exposed to different cultures, backgrounds, and races other than their own. They will benefit from having a culturally aware mindset. They will have more kindness toward and acknowledgment of people whose backgrounds are different from theirs, and they will be able to see how their actions and words affect the world around them. It is very dangerous for schools to neglect the social aspect of learning. This can lead to a world divided into different sections hating one another and continuing the widespread hatred we see today. Not promoting social growth in schools could let our youth of the world down because of the lack of awareness and education among and about other people in society.

SECOND

An emphasis on social awareness should not be separated from core subjects in the curriculum.

Core subjects should *not* exclude social aspects. Picture an English class where the teacher asks a student how they feel about a section in a nonfiction book, they give their opinion, and another student disagrees. The student who disagrees proceeds to make disrespectful remarks to the student who initially spoke, making that student uncomfortable, with both parties exhibiting nonverbal body language. Is the teacher not supposed to step in and let the student know why that was unacceptable? Could a teacher not provide advice on how the student could better handle disagreements? Being careless of the social upbringing of students could lead to a future of cold-bloodedness and malicious behavior. Wars have started due to a lack of humanity and understanding of people who look different or have a different background.

A lack of social intelligence learning impacted me in grammar school. Not only did I heat damage my hair trying to blend in, but I also had a harder time understanding why I felt the *need* to "blend in." In my schools, there were no Black teachers who taught me about representation. It wasn't until seventh grade that I met a teacher who was also a person of color. I wasn't ashamed of my culture, but I learned not to reveal certain parts of my culture. For example, I am half Jamaican, and curry chicken, goat, and other cultural dishes are staple foods. Seeing that other students were not eating the foods I grew up with made me feel that, if I wanted to blend in and not be picked on, sticking to pizza was the best option. Another example is that I had a friend in grammar school who was also African American and whose hair extensions fell out of her hair. Kids laughed and made fun of her. She was very shy afterward.

Some parents might say that these behaviors are just because kids are learning and growing. I say that's true. But when I was a senior in high school, staff and students were still running their hands through my curls while asking uncomfortable questions. These were people old enough to know to keep their hands to themselves unless consent was given for them to touch me, but my expectation of boundaries was something not everyone was taught, or they believed I would not mind this invasion of my personal space. But I very much minded. I still had to deal with classmates making the N-word into a joke. So, to say that social and emotional development should be taken out of schools is risky. Students should be able to feel comfortable going to school where they can laugh and be among fellow students of various backgrounds.

Sometimes, it is emotional intelligence that brings about significant change in the world. Whether it be a new invention to help underdeveloped areas or legislation to help those in need, our society requires a human connection to bring about change in the world. For example, think about when a natural disaster strikes a country; allies often send supplies and personnel to help those in need.

Blocking social and human connections in school is essentially blocking teachers from effectively doing their job. Some of the greatest teachers I had were the ones who picked up on their student's nonverbal language and would pull them aside to ask if everything was okay. Teachers who weren't "robots" and made jokes in class or shared stories about their dog and family vacation to the mountains. As a learner, I was more prone to listening to them lecture in class because they took the time to make us learners feel valued. School can be hard for students because they are going through changes in their lives and in their brain development. Yet the teachers who took time to build a positive connection with their students often had more respect from their students.

I ended up testing higher in those teachers' classes because I felt as though they cared about me. I wanted to make them proud of my academic success. In contrast, the teachers who kept a wall between them and their students, in my opinion, weren't easy to learn from. They had stone-cold faces, no reactions to anything, and overall were not pleasant to be around. It felt as though they wanted to be anywhere but in the classroom. While I still did well, I had to force myself to study and stay focused because I felt unwelcomed by the energy those teachers brought. Students rarely talked in those classes, and when they did many were meaner than in other settings.

Taking social and emotional intelligence out of schools is taking a part of the job that many students and teachers enjoy and need. I still remember my fourth-grade teacher, who was bright and happy every day at school. She cared about her students' social and emotional well-being. I don't forget that teachers like her made rough days better.

A core memory I have from PARU is the first few interviews we did. I remember being nervous to fully express how the book ban in our district affected me. As a learner in the district, I watered down my statements because I felt speaking out might affect my graduation or put me in serious trouble. But eventually, I was able to overcome that fear and really speak out along with the rest of the PARU board. We knew we had one another's backs in speaking out about our experiences in the district and about how this book ban made us feel as learners. Soon, Edha and I were called to speak at the Pennsylvania State Capitol where we met the members of the Black Caucus and then-Governor Tom Wolf. To say it feels refreshing to know PARU had support from our capital is an understatement. This support fueled us to keep going when the light at the end of the tunnel was distant.

Schools need social and emotional connection; students need to feel welcomed and appreciated in the place they are expected to learn and share. Taking out the social and emotional aspects of school is taking out a huge portion of what allows humans to connect. Nonverbal cues are essentially how the world is perceived by others. So why not allow schools and teachers to help to strengthen that skill in a controlled environment rather than the outside world? Based on my experience in American public school classrooms where social and emotional intelligence is promoted, students tend to do better because the teacher took the time to get to know and connect with them. Communication and people skills are sought in job applicants. People want others to care about them especially when they are in need. I hope to see a world where we embrace one another's differences with love and respect. I want to see that in school we address hard topics with sensitivity and care instead of just banning topics. It is selfish to take out social development from schools. What is the benefit of that? Don't let a few parents rob entire student bodies of having minds and opinions of their own. Humans need other humans' care and concern to survive. Let us allow our future generations to learn love and not hate.

WHAT TO SAY

When faced with the question of whether or not education should stick to core subjects, respond this way:

- **Students need to learn how to interact with others who are different from them.**
- **Core subjects benefit from an emphasis on social awareness in the curriculum.**

CHAPTER 8

DOES BRINGING UP DIVERSITY MAKE STUDENTS AND TEACHERS UNCOMFORTABLE?

Edha Gupta, president of PARU, 2021

In the wake of George Floyd's murder, the emergence of the Black Lives Matter movement, and Donald Trump's first presidential term, predominantly white school boards around the country started banning books. According to the American Library Association, "Between January 1 and August 31, 2024, ALA's Office for Intellectual Freedom tracked 414 attempts to censor library materials and services. In those cases, 1,128 unique titles were challenged. In the same reporting period last year, ALA tracked 695 attempts with 1,915 unique titles challenged" and "challenges of unique titles surged 65% in 2023 compared to 2022 numbers, reaching the highest level ever documented by ALA." This is a national crisis. It is not isolated; it is not unique.

Unite Against Book Bans reported that "47% of the books targeted for censorship were titles representing the voices and lived experiences of LGBTQIA+ and BIPOC individuals" in 2023. There are nationwide efforts to silence the voices of the marginalized.

I was seventeen years old when the Central York School District decided to ban over three hundred diversity resources in the district, but my education in the district started much earlier when I was enrolled at the Central York Panther Preschool. Although I grew up in a district with a lack of diversity education in the curriculum, no titles in the library had ever been *banned* in my thirteen years of schooling. So, in a district that claimed to nurture diversity and cultivate inclusion, how and why was censorship becoming so prevalent? Why did it matter so much now?

FIRST

I believe these bans across the country are reminiscent of nationwide attitudes about the marginalized communities in this country. There's a push to protect the status-quo of a whitewashed and nonsecular education in a formulaic way. White people are incentivized to protect the power they feel they are losing when marginalized voices are empowered. Ansley Erickson, associate professor of history and education policy at Columbia University, asserts that "the United States' history, since its inception, is full of uses of curriculum to shape politics, the economy and the culture. This is a really dramatic moment, but the curriculum has always been political, and people in power have always been using it to emphasize their power. And historically marginalized groups have always challenged that power."

The rise of attacks on diversity materials and curricula is no coincidence but a direct result of the rise of political polarization and the media's portrayal of topics such as critical race theory, diversity, equity, and inclusion, especially in recent years in America. I believe our school board became fearful about students being introduced to diversity materials. They assumed they, as white people, would be perceived as the perpetrators of oppression and villainized throughout the community. Ironically, instating this book ban reflected more poorly on them personally than anything in those materials.

This board saw the opportunity to make the curriculum align with their political beliefs, agenda, and personal beliefs about American history—whether or not they were conscious that they were doing this—and they took it. The political climate and polarization in America managed to infiltrate the education of a community. After George Floyd's murder, America was starting to talk about such things as white guilt, white fragility, systemic oppression, and BIPOC identity. This board did not want to entertain "uncomfortable" conversations like these.

SECOND

The *Oxford English Dictionary* defines *white guilt* as "remorse or shame felt by a white person concerning racial inequality and injustice." When the board saw this list of diversity resources, they did not see this list as pivotal in championing diversity, representation, and inclusion. It seemed as though they saw it as an attack on their character—as though they felt guilt for the country's racist past. It seemed that instead of acknowledging a racist national past through education, they wanted to ignore the existence of marginalized voices in literature. This guilt, combined with the need to "reobtain" the power they thought they were losing, is what I believe is the cause of so many book bans around the country today.

By banning these books, the board constructed the narrative that microaggressions and racist experiences in a student's life did not deserve to be talked about nor validated. Whether they wanted to or not, they sent the message to the Central York community that marginalized voices were not *important* enough to be heard and, therefore, should be banned from classrooms.

For me, this journey started in March 2021, when I was chosen to join a Zoom session to talk to all the then current board members about the state of diversity education and representation in the district. Here, I expressed to them that the diversity education that I had received in my thirteen years of schooling in the district had been lackluster—and I told them *why*. I explained the racist comments I would get daily and the microaggressions that I endured. I explained how not seeing a book with a girl that looked like me had a detrimental impact on my perception of myself, my identity, and my journey in loving myself. While they seemed receptive to my constructive criticism, the ban was instated six months later at the will of some board members and parents. When the ban came out, it felt like a slap in the face.

I was an example of the negative consequences that not having access to adequate representation could have on kids. I learned about slavery for two weeks—but about the American Revolution (1775–1783) from seventh grade to ninth grade. I was one of the few brown girls who populated my grade and therefore felt deep shame about my culture and identity from a young age. In annual diversity celebrations when I would dance to Bollywood music, I would be sent videos of my performances and mocked for my cultural attire and dance.

At these celebrations, peers would make disgusted looks at our family henna stand, and I was told to "go back to my country" multiple times in a week. I grew up in a culturally insensitive and hostile environment. As a Hindu Indian American girl, I made efforts to erase any part of me in school that was reminiscent of my Indian identity. I started laughing at the Indian accents people would mock, and I started being tolerant to casual racism and microaggressions. I craved to be white. I craved to be "normal." I craved to be accepted. I wanted my personhood to be validated, but my skin color communicated something before my words had the chance to.

My white peers would never *see* me, *understand* me, or *appreciate* me as I wanted them to. I was exhausted, and I was angry. The sense of "normalcy" I wanted to attain throughout my thirteen years of education in this district was *never attainable*, and I had to do something about it.

This ban symbolized what this school board stood for—everything that was antithetical to fostering a safe space for marginalized students and making them feel represented in their schooling. Although proponents of the ban argued the ban on books written by Dr. Suess, *Sesame Street* episodes on diversity, a book about a Black girl learning to love her hair, and three hundred others were not made available to *reduce* division between students and the community, marginalized and diverse students became outsiders in their schooling. School was *never* a safe space for me, and it would not be before I graduated. I resigned myself to that. But I could not resign myself to this cycle of self-hatred and assimilation being reinforced for generations of marginalized students to come. I did not want them to go through what I had to.

Mobilized by our collective surprise at the blatant disrespect that we felt, PARU gathered the night that the article about the school board's decision was published in the *York Dispatch*. We started with a blackout the Friday after we were aware of the decision. Students who were against the book ban came in droves wearing black to show their support to have the books put back in the library. The Monday after, we started protesting in front of the school with signs saying, *Education Is Not Indoctrination* and *My Voice Matters*.

Activism then became a part-time job with PARU members continually speaking at board meetings, organizing community protests, working at book drives, and speaking to the media to get the ban reversed and the books back in the library. In our outreach, we reassured a generation of voices that thought they were incapable of making change that not only were they capable—but they were directly responsible for catalyzing it. By the end of our two weeks of protesting, we had at least thirty to forty kids standing outside the Central York High School every day.

Before the ban, I would have not thought it was within my *bounds* to protest a book ban. As a first-generation daughter of immigrants, Indian American, and "*model minority*" woman, I had always worked hard to conform to the roles others wanted to assign to me. My close friends and family were confused by my moral prerogative to protest—what everyone in my immediate community thought was a radical act that would spur severe disciplinary consequences.

The term "model minority" is a harmful stereotype that describes a minority group as having a higher socioeconomic status than the general population.

What I was doing was uncharacteristic for other girls my age in the Indian American community—it was *unheard of.* But it always came back to these questions: If not us, who? If not now, when? I couldn't wait and hope—none of us could. For the first time, I disobeyed. For the first time in my educational career, I disregarded the disciplinary consequences or negative public response—I was motivated by the need for justice for myself and all the other marginalized students in this district who had the misfortune of learning an incomplete history.

So, we started speaking to news outlets: CNN, *The Washington Post, The New York Times, The Guardian*, Yahoo, the *Daily Mail*, and the list goes on. People in our local community and around the country were invested in this issue and wanted to see us prevail. Community members showed up in large numbers to protests, and teachers and supporters all over the country donated to Amazon wish lists that we used to continue the work of anti-racism and representation within PARU in subsequent years. The support was inspiring. Community members organized a book drive where hundreds of books were donated and given to the Central York community. Our group spoke to Congress, congressional representatives, senators, and governors; gave a TED Talk; and was on *The Kelly Clarkson Show*. We have received honors such as the Beloved Community Awards from the King Center and have met inspiring activists from around the country.

Marketing for TEDxPenn's 2022 Affect Conference.

Being a junior in a university has immensely widened my perspective. The representation that I craved in my primary schooling and fought for is now easily accessible to me. I sit in classes such as sociology of gender, listening to other college students talk about the detailed discussions and curricula they were introduced to in their elementary and secondary education, including the Stonewall riots, Frederick Douglass, and the Selma to Montgomery march. These students hold a wealth of knowledge that was never truly accessible to me. The students of Central were fed a false narrative: that comfort lies in intolerance.

I have conversations in academic settings that before were framed to me as radical, divisive, and polarizing. It took me eighteen years to feel safe in a classroom while listening to a peer talk about her experience of coming out or another Indian girl talk about the adversity she faced. *These students did not have to learn that it is empowering to take ownership over their identities.* My professors have cultivated this type of discussion and work hard to validate these students. A generation of students who grow up and are taught narratives of history from a predetermined agenda are being robbed of their full potential—banning educational materials actively hurts the youth of this country. When we talk about loving our students, it means to entrust the youth with the future of this country. This means working in their best interests. We need to do that through giving them the *full story*. School boards operating from a political or social agenda are operating from a flawed set of values.

The book ban was reversed after two weeks of consistent advocacy through arranging school-wide and community-wide protests, book distributions, speaking at weekly school board meetings and, most important, drawing attention to this critical issue in the community. Advocacy is a pillar of society and integral to change. As young people, we are at the precipice of calamity in so many ways, and this can be daunting but also inspiring. There is a sense of assurance, calm, and self-gratification when we take autonomy over building a better future for ourselves and those around us. Through this journey of personal and collective advocacy, we have catalyzed a need for never-ending advocacy within all of us—a flame that will keep burning no matter where I am or what I do. Representative, holistic, diverse, and inclusive education is a *human right*. This is sadly a human right that we as students need to fight for and ferociously protect. We are told far too often that we are too uneducated, naive, or young to make tangible impacts on society.

If you are being told this narrative as a student or as a young person, *know that it is not true*. My narrative empowered me to make a tangible impact in my community, and yours has the power to do so too. If you see book banning and attacks on equitable and representative resources or education happening in your community—speak up. Use the power of your voice to stand up for yourself and your community. Look for school board meetings and attend them. Speak to local legislators about censorship and meet with your peers to hear about their thoughts and perspectives on these issues. You are never alone.

Central York School District's mission statement says that they provide learners with a "high-quality academic experience within a supportive, valued, collaborative community that promotes students' personal growth and the pursuit of their passions and interests." I would've loved to attend a Central where this mission was truly accomplished. With our advocacy, I know that it will be.

WHAT TO SAY

When faced with the question of whether or not bringing up diversity makes students and teachers uncomfortable, respond this way:

- **These bans across the country are reminiscent of nationwide attitudes about the marginalized communities in this country.**
- **The study of diversity is not an attack on anyone's character that implies guilt for the country's racist past. Diversity adds a new lens with which to view the past.**

CHAPTER 9

ARE HIGH SCHOOL STUDENTS MATURE ENOUGH TO HANDLE CHALLENGING SUBJECT MATTER?

Ben Hodge, founder and co-adviser of PARU

When I started teaching, I thought I was going to be a strict teacher who operated by control and discipline. That's what I was taught to be. Undergrad training was all about standards, curriculum, lesson planning, and assessment. While classroom management was the buzzword at the time, there was little to no practical training or preparation in how to navigate, understand, and effectively *reach* the students that I would be teaching. There was no preparation for the stories of homelessness, abuse, neglect, and trauma that twenty-first-century students face.

Like many young teachers, I had to figure it out on the fly. Perhaps this is why teacher retention rates are so bad these days. A 2022 survey by the National Education Association found that 55 percent of teachers said they were considering leaving the profession. In many instances, teachers are ill-prepared to walk into a classroom of students who all have distinct personalities, learning styles, and life experiences. Somehow, in the midst of all of that diversity, a community of learning must be built. A key step to success in any classroom is fostering a space where kids can feel safe and courageous to be who they are so they can learn effectively. An element of trust needs to be developed between the teacher and student. But what happens when students are not believed to be trustworthy or capable of meeting high expectations?

One of the major arguments that we heard during our fight against the book ban was that the material needed to be banned because the students couldn't handle the content in the books. This argument implies that high school students (grades 9–12) are not mature or "adult" enough to handle particularly challenging and complex subject matter. In other words, they cannot be trusted to deal with this type of material.

I found this to be quite common among community members, administrators, and some faculty members: They look at their students as children and not young adults. Instead of entrusting them and guiding them through *how* to think, proponents of this argument codify teachers to only tell students *what* to think, primarily with a standardized test as the sole assessment.

FIRST

High school students should be treated as young adults rather than children.

In many ways, being a teenager hasn't changed that much over the years. Today's teenagers, like previous generations, navigate schoolwork, postsecondary prep, busy social calendars, part-time jobs, and extracurricular activities all while being a part of a family unit. However, I've still heard many adults say, "Teens have it so easy now." But the statistics tell a different story. You don't have to look too far for the data to see the toll these busy schedules has taken. Many researchers believe that our teens are facing a mental health crisis. Some of the numbers are staggering: According to Clarify Health, youth mental health hospitalizations increased by 124 percent from 2016 to 2022. An estimated 31.9 percent of teens are diagnosed with an anxiety disorder, and 20 percent of teens will experience depression by the age of seventeen with girls twice as likely as boys to have clinical depression. These young people may have more opportunities and activities, but it is coming at a cost.

Any teenager can attest to how much they love their technology. The same study said that teenagers spend an average of seven hours and twenty-two minutes daily on their screens. Of course, the access to technology and information has made life easier and more efficient in many ways, but it also sets up a situation where we are constantly "connected" to one another via social media and our technology. This is a wonderful thing for keeping in touch and communicating with family and friends but damaging as well because young students can't really get away from the drama. When I was a student, if I faced bullying or a problematic relationship at school, it would often be known by me and a handful of others. These days, the likelihood of many *more* people being in one another's business is so much higher. Many students have trouble escaping the cycle of trauma and drama because it is constantly looped on social media and in virtual social circles.

Early on in my teacher prep, very little time was spent on preparing me for understanding and guiding students through their lived experiences and personal trauma. There is an unfortunate and devastating implicit expectation for many teachers: that students inherently will walk into your classroom able to "check their baggage at the door," and get right down to the learning. If only it were true.

The truth is no significant learning can really happen in a classroom if the students' minds are mired in conflict, trauma, personal drama, or more than one of these. It doesn't matter how passionate I am or how exciting the content or lesson is. I first realized this back in 2008 when I challenged my students to compose a play about their lives called *Reach*. The concept in itself was simple: I asked them to turn a mirror on the school and tell the *real* stories of what was going on at Central York High School. The result of their work was a two-act play that told stories of divorce, self-harm, substance abuse, sexual assault, bullying, race identity, and academic stress. I can remember being shocked and saying multiple times to many of the students, "Is this what it is really like for you all?" Their answer was a solemn "Yes, Hodge. No one has ever really asked us about it. Everyone just assumes we are here to learn and that's it."

This was a wake-up call for me. After *Reach*, I began to see my students differently: not just as pupils in my classroom receiving my content but as complex human beings with resilience, grit, and determination. I realized that they were calling out to me for more challenging material and a deeper sense of respect and authenticity. They wanted to be treated like adults, not as little kids. Their stories had shown me that.

Fast-forward twelve years, and the students of PARU were echoing that same refrain: Treat us like young adults, not kids. During the 2020–2021 book ban, the board continued to argue that high school students shouldn't have access to challenging material centered on race, identity, and diversity. Yet these were the things that the students were grappling with. The students were frustrated with this argument because when you spoke to them, they would talk about how they *wanted* to learn and talk about the racial reckoning that was occurring. Yet this ban effectively made the discussion taboo or untouchable in school.

SECOND

Denying access to culturally relevant and topical content stunts students' intellectual, personal, and mental health growth.

As a theater teacher, it has become evident in my work with teen actors that my students are deeply interested in stories that are engaging, relatable, and authentic. When I first started teaching, most of the content I used in my class was teacher determined. I would select work and pieces that I wanted to perform or that interested me. I remember the students receiving the material somewhat tentatively, with limited excitement or engagement. After my transformational *Reach* experience, I discovered that the students were hungry for a deeper personal connection to their art and work. I began to encourage students to look for material that *they* were interested in performing and stories that *they* were interested in telling. The stories they selected often proved to be deeper and more "mature" than I expected they wanted. These stories were about loss, identity, navigating life, and hope for a better world. My students were capable of handling challenging material because they were living challenging circumstances each day.

During my comments at protests, board meetings, and interviews with the media, I began to share some of these findings, imploring that students benefit from wrestling with the challenging concepts of identity, lived experiences, and trauma. My students often tell me that my classroom is one of the only places where they "can be themselves" or "really feel that no one is judging them for who they are." I would invite these students to share their poems and artwork with people at the board meetings and rallies with the sole intent to force people to hear that their stories are *real* and *authentic*. These stories helped our school board and other members of the community realize that our students are not just kids. They are young adults who are experiencing a myriad of real-world issues that they need to process and learn about to grow and develop.

When any district bans resources and materials focused on "challenging concepts," it is denying growth and learning to its student population. My students are inquisitive and resourceful. They want to engage with real-world conversation and content. When they are told they can't handle specific content, many of them scoff and say things like "They don't really know me" or "Why don't they trust us? Don't they know we see and live this stuff every day?" Denying access to a resource about microaggressions or racism doesn't protect kids from danger. It denies the students who are living it every day an opportunity to understand what is happening to them and how they can successfully navigate it. Banning a book that speaks about sexual assault doesn't shield students from experiencing it. It eliminates the opportunity to see that they are not alone. Not every student may be interested in reading those concepts, but we must remember that some of our students (especially in public school settings) *will* be interested.

One of my students, Eva, said: "I use books to escape my own world . . . when I read books that 'hit close to home' I feel more connected and reassured. I don't talk about things that I went through so when I'm reading a book I feel as though I'm talking through the character . . . or I can have 'someone' to relate to and it honestly makes me feel better." Eva gets to the point here: Books and stories can lead to a connection to and a deeper understanding of lived experiences.

Why would anyone want to deny self-awareness and self-efficacy? Students need to see themselves in the material they are reading, and we need to stop being naive about their lived experiences. I believe that my students are fully capable of dealing with more challenging topics because I have heard about the challenging life experiences they live with daily. I hope we all start to actually listen to them.

WHAT TO SAY

When faced with the question of whether or not high school students are mature enough to handle challenging subject matter, respond this way:

- **High school students should be treated as young adults rather than children.**
- **Denying access to culturally relevant and topical content stunts students' intellectual, personal, and mental health growth.**

CHAPTER 10

IS FRANK DISCUSSION ABOUT SEX THE SAME AS PORNOGRAPHY?

Patricia A. Jackson, co-adviser of PARU

Famous essayist and social activist James Baldwin said, "The purpose of education is to create in a person the ability to look at the world for himself, to make his own decisions." As the 2020 Central York Board of Directors seemed to undermine this tenet by scaring teachers away from discussing any issues of social justice or current events, I couldn't help but wonder, Did these elected officials fear the content being taught in our district? Or did they fear the outcome of young people critically thinking and making decisions for themselves?

Sitting in yet another public meeting where the board bashed the district's teachers and accused us of indoctrination and political subversion, I believed the situation could not get any more absurd. I was wrong. During the citizen comment period allotted during board meetings for community members to speak directly to the board,

James Baldwin, American essayist, author, and civil rights advocate has been a major inspiration for the Panther Anti-Racist Union and others. His sharp wit and honest analysis were prophetic and compelling.

one outspoken community member announced that she had reported the district to the Springettsbury Township Police Department for distributing pornography to children! She had taken a copy of George M. Johnson's memoir *All Boys Aren't Blue* to the police as evidence.

As mentioned in a previous chapter, when media scrutiny increased, the board shifted their tactics and attacked not just books by and about people in the LGBTQIA+ community but students who identified as being part of this marginalized community. This included the removal of books and resources, as well as threats to roll back rights for transgender students with regard to preferred names and pronouns. They felt safe in doing so because their staunchest supporter was a right-wing lesbian who referred to these kids as crybabies and clowns who needed to "get over themselves because life is just hard." She failed to see that portraying the literature of this community as pornography was dangerous.

Dozens of students from PARU and the Beautiful People, a gender/sexuality alliance club at the high school, came to the board meeting to speak against the book ban, the board's discriminatory stance against them and, in particular, the hateful rhetoric against transgender students. Along with the book ban, there was a movement by a male member of the school board to reverse bathroom privileges for trans students, even if it meant losing federal monies. This would mean a trans student would no longer be allowed to use the bathroom that corresponded to their gender identity.

One young man from the club spoke about the book *All Boys Aren't Blue* and how the novel gave him the courage to confide in a parent about how he had been repeatedly sexually assaulted by a family member when he was younger. "That book saved my life," he told the board. I was so proud of him!

Meanwhile, Hannah Shipley, a friend of PARU and a local TikTok content creator, was under siege from people who adhered to the board's beliefs. They attacked her via social media and accused her of giving out pornography to kids at a local book distribution where four thousand "banned" books were made available to the Central York community. This disruptive but faceless minority called for her to be officially charged.

Fortunately, nothing ever came of those threats, and the police department referred the disgruntled community member back to the school board. Despite the absurdity of the claim, this didn't stop certain members of the board and their supporters from insisting Johnson's hard-hitting memoir was pornography, and they were determined to prove it. I was equally determined to prove them wrong!

FIRST

The terms "pornography" and "obscenity" are often applied to books targeted for banning. But these books don't meet the legal definition of obscene materials established by the US Supreme Court. The court case *Miller v. California* 413 U.S. 15 (1973), frequently referred to as the Miller Test, says that the basis of obscenity must include these three criteria:

- "The average person, applying contemporary community standards" would find that the work, "taken as a whole," appeals to the "prurient interest" (*prurient* means "to encourage excessive interest in sexual activity").
- The work depicts or describes, in a patently offensive way, sexual conduct specifically defined by the applicable state law.
- The work, "taken as a whole," lacks serious literary, artistic, political, or scientific value.

People in favor of book bans never interpret the law unless it is in their favor. The board failed to examine these works as a whole. Instead, they chose specific passages to invoke a visceral response from the community. Allowing children to read difficult or mature content is an ideal opportunity for parents or guardians to have a candid conversation with their kids and establish safe boundaries. But in the Central York School District, the term *pornography* was used as a dog whistle from the right-wing playbook to frighten parents and whip the school community into a fervor.

This was the case with the novel *Push*, which would subsequently be removed from the high school library under a parental challenge. The merits of the book were boiled down to its vernacular: the halted, broken speech of an illiterate Black girl, as masterfully captured by the author, Sapphire. Comparing this style to the literary quality of Laura Esquivel's novel *Like Water for Chocolate*, an approved novel in the English curriculum, a colleague parsed it down to the simple use of words: breasts vs. titties.

She voted to remove *Push* and pointed out the use of the word *titties* as evidence of the novel's lack of literary merit as opposed to the word *breasts* used in *Like Water for Chocolate*. This veteran teacher argued that the distinctive languages of the novels was like comparing apples and oranges. When debating the depiction of intimate sexual intercourse on a horse in the Esquivel novel versus the sexual assault of a child in the other, she argued the latter was too graphic, less skillful.

The vernacular of *Push* was raw, unapologetic, and Black, so the novel was deemed unworthy of literary merit, while the highly stylistic language and magical realism of *Like Water for Chocolate* got a pass for being artful. Depictions of sexual activity, even rape, could be condoned as literary in certain books, such as the novel *Sold* by Patricia McCormick. For me, it was further evidence of the racial divide in the community, particularly among educators, quibbling over the semantics of breasts and titties, without evaluating the context to validate the banning of a library book.

The United States has not just a race problem but a Black problem. I believe that the moment Black characters entered the equation, the work is often fetishized, demonized, and labeled pornographic.

My colleague refused to see that *Push* excelled, not only in literary excellence for its authentic depiction of language but also in political commentary on mental health and the staggering lack of care offered to victims of sexual assault. The novel's authenticity did not fall into any literary genre as defined by white spaces, so it was reduced to the label of pornography.

SECOND

Many survivors of sexual assault connect with characters in such books. The cruel scrutiny that can come with revealing the truth makes it difficult for victims to come forward with accounts of sexual abuse. As a survivor of sexual assault, I can attest that suppressing, dismissing, or erasing the experiences of victims is often worse than the harm perpetrated on them by their violation. Many suffer in silence without getting proper help because they fear the stigma and judgment more than they fear the abuser.

These survivors find lifesaving connections to the characters in such books. Through the protagonist's journey, which may mirror their experiences, victims find their own courage to process the abuse, identify their perpetrators, and get the help they desperately need to heal.

More important, survivors may find acceptance, without judgment, in a community of others who intimately understand their pain. The banning of such books erases the voices of victims, displacing them and their stories, and removing them from where they can be the most helpful. This can reaffirm to victims that they are unwelcomed, unwanted, and need to be hidden away from society or removed like the books. Sexual assault must never be interpreted as pornographic, rather than a violent attack on one's humanity.

Student readers often refer to books as the safe places they can carry with them, places where they wrestle with their feelings, inner demons, and doubts alongside the protagonists struggling to find happily ever after. The life experiences within the pages are not always unique because they frequently mirror the best and the worst of the human experience. Ultimately, the reader returns from their journey with new knowledge and a sense that they are not alone, not weird, not bizarre. Pornography, by its scripted, artificial nature, can never achieve this.

No matter how hard we might try, teachers, parents, guardians, or other adults cannot protect kids from the harsh realities of life. When we isolate and insulate them from truth, we leave them more vulnerable to the pitfalls of living and fail to give them the necessary tools to properly engage in the real world beyond the comfort and safety of their living rooms, sports stadiums, and classrooms.

WHAT TO SAY

When faced with the question of whether frank discussion about sex is the same as pornography, respond this way:

- **The books being challenged do not fit the legal definition of pornography or obscenity.**
- **Many survivors of sexual assault connect with characters in such books.**

CHAPTER 11

SHOULD KIDS LEARN ABOUT THE LGBTQIA+ COMMUNITY?

Olivia Pituch, secretary and social media adviser for PARU

The Trevor Project is the largest suicide prevention nonprofit organization for LGBTQIA+ youth in the United States. They spread awareness about LGBTQIA+ youth, have a hub of various ways a person can receive help, and even offer an "easy escape" to leave the website for those who could be in danger if caught viewing the pages. Not only have I admired their work for years, but I had the pleasure of participating on a panel with people from the Trevor Project. The experience confirmed what I already knew: The organization was doing life-altering work.

FIRST

LGBTQIA+ youth exist with or without exposure to the community.

Some people believe organizations like the Trevor Project

are the cause of LGBTQIA+ individuals' existence, instead of the result. They believe that the feelings of the LGBTQIA+ community would not exist among youth if they are not told about these feelings.

This false argument is fascinating. A few of my best friends, for example, enjoy LGBTQIA+ books such as *Heartstopper* and *Red, White, and Royal Blue*, yet they have remained straight. If "exposure" to sexualities forces those feelings onto you, I should be "straight!" A heterosexual, cisgender default has surrounded me in every aspect of my life. Movies, books, my own family, math problems; everything paired a boy with a girl. The concept was forced down my throat.

The popular *Heartstopper* series of graphic novels by author Alice Oseman has faced book bans nationwide.

For a while, I didn't know you could date someone of the same sex. Despite this, I was always pulled toward girls while growing up. I was confused by the funny little butterflies filling my stomach when a beautiful girl came on-screen. I got nervous around girls I found especially pretty, and when my friends who were girls held my hand to lead me somewhere on the playground, my heart would soar. I was not introduced to the LGBTQIA+ community until

I already had years of experience with these feelings. The first time I really had experience with the community was when I did the musical *Rent* at a local theater in the summer before ninth grade. I felt so bubbly every time I saw the characters Maureen and Joanne loving each other so openly. It was during this show that I kissed a girl for the first time. At the time, it was just my friends and me playing around, so I didn't think it was a big deal. But I thought about that kiss for months.

Being deprived of learning about the LGBTQIA+ community did not save me from being gay just as only seeing straight couples did not "turn me" straight. It only confused, ostracized, and limited me for years. Banning LGBTQIA+ books will not make all children straight and cisgender. It will only make closeted students' journeys painful. Being integrated into the community is ultimately what saved me. It helped me understand, navigate, and accept these feelings.

I began seeking books with characters who were like me to affirm the experiences I never had the nerve to relay aloud. The isolation brought on by the pandemic allowed me to lean into what made me happy and comfortable rather than the social norms pushed onto students in a school environment. My experience is not uncommon. I have heard countless coming-out stories that closely align with mine. Stories about how young girls wanting to play a "dad" in family games so they could be with a girl, stories about boys asking why they can't marry or love the boy from school, kids being drawn to clothing that isn't typically worn by their gender. Most of the time, these feelings originate on their own and without prompting from LGBTQIA+ media. Allowing kids access to the LGBTQIA+ community through these books does not "create gay people." It often helps those within the community to find their way.

SECOND

When kids are introduced to differences early on, they are more accepting of themselves and others.

Today's society is one where it is increasingly common to have a child with LGBTQIA+ parents or family. This means that having inclusive education and LGBTQIA+ representation is important. Having math word problems that contain different kinds of parents can be beneficial. One problem could talk about Johnny's two dads, while another can talk about Jessica's mom and dad. Constantly portraying only one type of family creates the idea that the family portrayed is the only correct or normal family. Even portraying single parents or foster families can be beneficial. The more these families are seen in normal settings, such as word problems or read-aloud books, the more accepted and "normal" they become. People can react negatively to things that are different, new, or unexplained. When the frequency of inclusion is high, people are less likely to bat an eye at the things that were once different and scary.

For kids, inclusion is essential. It's much easier to learn than it is to unlearn. Unlearning implies the need to shed old concepts and ways of thinking. It means ridding your mind of the things you believed to be correct. This is incredibly hard. Unlearning only gets more difficult as time goes by. That's why it is so important to allow kids to learn acceptance from a young age. Teaching kids to be accepting and allowing them to learn that not every family will look the same creates a loving and safe community. The first step in fostering that safe space is to *allow* LGBTQIA+ books in classrooms, libraries, and students' hands.

Promoting inclusivity creates healthier, happier environments for all children. LGBTQIA+ representation and literature in schools does not mean trying to convince children that they are part of the LGBTQIA+ community. It means normalizing same-sex and different-sex couples in the same way. It means representing that families can have two moms, two dads, one mom, a dad and a mom, one dad, or a different family group. It means instead of heterosexuality as the stated normal, other forms of love are also viewed as normal.

THIRD

Heteronormativity is a learned concept.

LGBTQIA+ children exist, regardless of how exposed they are to the community. This is not what makes a child consider their own gender and sexuality. Having access to other members of their community (people of similar sexual orientations or gender identities) can help them become more assured and comfortable in their own skin. It is so affirming for young people questioning their sexuality to know they're not alone. Navigating those emotions and feelings is extremely difficult.

LGBTQIA+ books can educate young children so that they grow up welcoming of *all* people and steer *all* youth toward being themselves rather than being forced into societal stereotypes. Even if you aren't queer, you can feel confined by a perpetuated norm. These books are about embracing your identity and who you are, even if it's a little different.

We are exposed to heteronormativity from the start. Our understanding of it is learned. Although kids' shows are beginning to incorporate very accepting concepts, such as having same-sex parents, the moment we can process thoughts, we are constantly having heteronormativity modeled for us. Adults ship little boys and girls, talking about which children would make the cutest heteronormative couple. Books generally contain boys loving girls and girls loving boys. Shows, with the exception of some newer ones, have mom and dad parents. Kids are exposed to all of this, and no one bats an eye. Even young girls having to play the dad to be with another girl in games shows how deeply rooted heteronormativity is in society. This is all learned. Kids are born accepting and loving and prone to following their feelings naturally. They are taught the rest.

Some people believe that LGBTQIA+ affirmation is inherently sexual and inappropriate, but that is not true. It means telling children that they can love and marry whomever they want to. It means showing parents consisting of two moms or two dads. It means having books where a girl begins to get nervous around another girl. It means keeping all the concepts and age-appropriate content the same—just adding inclusivity.

I had the opportunity to be a part of a pride video with Senator Bob Casey (D-PA). Not only was I thrilled when I found out he wanted to do a pride video, but finding out he wanted PARU involved was so healing. My sexuality journey was still fairly fresh, and it felt so incredible to be in a video celebrating my identity. I want every child to experience feeling proud, comfortable, and loved in their identity. I want every child to see and love every part of themselves. I want every child not to be ostracized because of their identity. I want every child to learn acceptance and see their identity normalized, not hated. LGBTQIA+ representation does not create LGBTQIA+ children.

It saves them.

WHAT TO SAY

When faced with the question of whether or not kids should learn about the LGBTQIA+ community, respond this way:

- **LGBTQIA+ youth exist with or without exposure to the community.**
- **When kids are introduced to differences early on, they are more accepting of themselves and others.**
- **Heteronormativity is a learned concept.**

CHAPTER 12

WILL READING BOOKS WITH SENSITIVE SUBJECT MATTER MAKE CHILDREN DO WHAT THEY'RE READING ABOUT?

Edha Gupta, president of PARU, 2021

I remember the first time I was taught about civil rights. I was in a ninth-grade classroom. For the first time, I was introduced to the whitewashed version of America's racist past. I learned about the transatlantic slave trade and read the "Letter from Montgomery Jail." Although what I was taught was not wholly representative of the atrocities committed against Black people in America, it helped me develop a baseline level of understanding and empathy for Black culture and community.

Studying civil rights for just a week changed my viewpoint of America and my place in it. So, when I heard that the same history that enriched my life and provided me with empathy toward my peers was *dividing* white students, I did not believe it. This knowledge did not turn me against my peers but rather it raised questions about the implications of my identity—specifically, the meaning of it in relation to my social dynamics with others.

Since that time in my life, my knowledge of civil rights has exponentially grown, and it informs so much of my perception and my knowledge about my life. Knowing about systemic barriers faced by marginalized people in America aids me in engaging in acts of resistance to dismantle oppressive systems and ways of thinking (such as protesting censorship of books). Watching this book ban agenda gain traction in our district showed me the real culprit of division and resentment in students.

The year when two new books, *A Court of Mist and Fury* by Sarah J. Maas and *Push* by Sapphire, were taken out of the Central York Library, several board members and members of the community argued that books that talked about nuanced experiences of marginalized communities were divisive. Although these books contained mature content, the primary readership of these books remained teenagers. My question was, When did we decide that comfort equated to good schooling? Shouldn't good schooling *challenge* students? Shouldn't it make them think about the world differently? Shouldn't it challenge the previously held perspectives that students have? Isn't that the real purpose of education?

Push had been in the library since 1996. (I guess until then Central York had a different definition of "good education"—one that I could maybe agree with.) *A Court of Mist and Fury* was banned for sexual content, and *Push* was about a young girl navigating life after enduring physical and mental abuse from her mother and sexual abuse from her father. Although these books did have challenging content, banning them without community or faculty support was unjust and invalidating to students who have gone through experiences similar to Precious—the main character in *Push*. Banning these books told students with similar life experiences to characters in these books that their life experiences was "too divisive" to be included in a school library. Isn't it *more* divisive to have an unrepresentative library filled with just one type of story or perspective? It did not make sense to ban these books and justify

The popular book *A Court of Mist and Fury* by Sarah J. Maas was banned in the Central York School District for "sexual content."

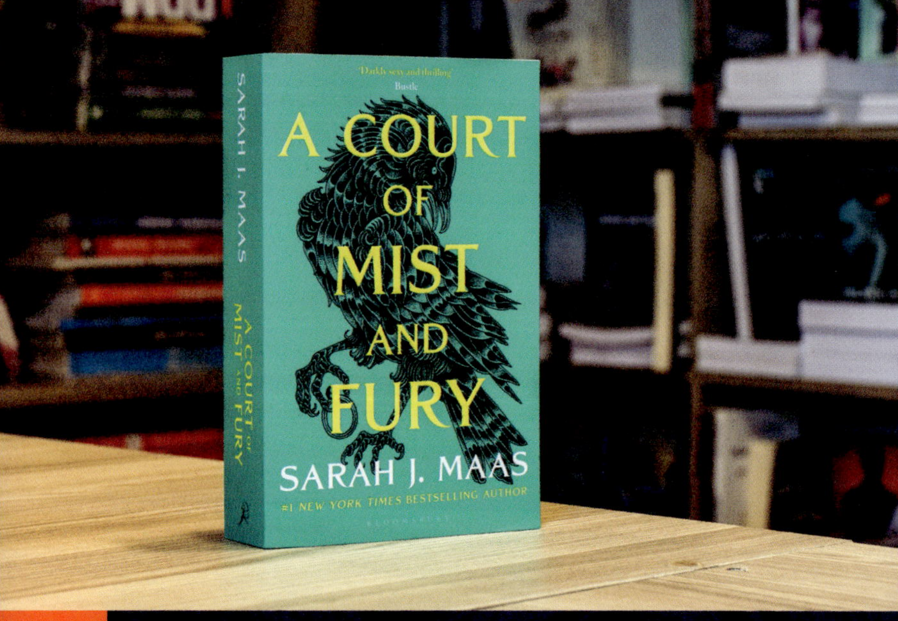

it by claiming to decrease the divide. I believe these bans were made to *increase comfort* for the book banners. Let's unpack their arguments.

FIRST

Banning these books set the precedent at Central that because a book has triggering material or even controversial material, it should be restricted for students. The all-white school board was allowed unlimited power to be the deciders of what was acceptable to be put in school libraries. Unsurprisingly, the books and resources these people supported only reflected their narrow perception of the world and their own role in it. I'm left to wonder if, in some way, access to material depicting such systems as colonialism, imperialism, and slavery made these board members feel they were being *blamed* for these things and they were personally being framed as racists or bigots. If that were the case, these board members might have only been concerned with their own images within the community. And because those images may have affected their reelection, they may have been unable to challenge their own implicit racism.

As a student who has not gone through what Precious had gone through in *Push*, I believe that books such as this can help students who haven't gone through the same experiences to empathize and learn about the world around them. I believe that the most sacred types of knowledge are gathered from empathy for and emotional understanding of others. Love is the glue that holds humanity together, and empathy allows love to flourish. We need to start loving our students enough to educate them holistically. By depriving students of books with sensitive material, I feel this board was showing to the Central York community that it cared more about its comfort than its students' inclusion.

As an Indian American girl who felt unrepresented in my schooling, instances of racism and hatred have scarred me for life and hurt me in ways from which I am still healing. Empathy is the lifeblood of society. It is a pillar in everyday life and social well-being. It is integral to forming relationships with people and fostering love in our communities. It is critical.

SECOND

Framing books that document the real experiences that students face as disgusting is invalidating, hurtful, and distasteful. I know that reading books that document the real experiences of students increases my compassion and empathy, and I will continue to engage with uncomfortable, critical literature and people as I move throughout academia. That is one of the purposes of education. Stories have served powerful roles in my life. Some stories have made me feel uncomfortable, and some have reaffirmed my perceptions of the world. I have never been *worse* off by being *more* educated. If love is the glue that builds this society together, stories constitute love. Stories do not perpetuate divisiveness; people do. Stories do not make children unkind; people do. Blaming the books for the increasing levels of hate in this world is doing everyone a disservice.

Children are the future changemakers, leaders, and influencers. We can do so much for them by allowing them to access an education that is not already fractured by polarization and hate. It is time to tell our stories louder, and it is time to start to love. Books are not the representations of hate but rather the physical, tangible manifestations of love. Reading more, learning more, and educating more is the direct path to a just, equitable society.

WHAT TO SAY

When faced with the question of whether or not reading books with sensitive material can make children do what they're reading about, respond this way:

- **Books such as this can help students who haven't gone through the same experiences to empathize and learn about the world around them.**
- **Framing books that document the real experiences that students face as disgusting is invalidating, hurtful, and distasteful.**

CHAPTER 13

ARE DIVERSITY RESOURCES ANTI-RELIGIOUS?

PART 1

Renee Ellis, former director of communications and outreach and former president of PARU

As we grow older, we all must decide who we are. No one can make the decision for us; rather we must assemble the characteristics, mannerisms, and beliefs that will define and shape how we present to the world.

One important decision to make is to decide whether you will have a faith or religion and what it will be. When growing up, I was taught not to speak on two things: religion and politics. Those two topics have been the cause of division for many years. People will defend to their dying day their political beliefs, their religious faith, or both. As a society, we are so passionate about these issues because they are so important in our personal lives. They are symbolic of our beliefs and morals.

I am a Christian. But I believe a relationship with God is

more important than religion. My faith in God and a relationship with God means more to me than rituals or tasks. But we all have a different connection to faith or religion. We follow different religions, and some of us choose not to follow a religion or faith. Everyone and every religion deserves respect, inclusion, representation, and equality.

Discrimination against someone based on their religious beliefs is illegal but also wrong and dangerous. Resources about different religious groups and cultures help us to understand and appreciate others' beliefs, but some people have created the narrative that diversity resources are anti-religious. Some parents believe that if their children learn about different religions, they are forsaking the religion they want them to have. But every child needs to decide for themselves what they believe. No teacher, author, or book can or should sway a child from what they truly believe. And every child should learn to be respectful of other religions.

FIRST

Books about different religions teach us how to respect one another.

I have moved more times than I can remember, but I've always remembered the people that I have met. I've learned so much about life and how to live it just by being able to meet so many people. When I lived in Ohio, I attended Orchard Middle School. There I had a friend group that I will never forget. We used to do everything together. It was like the Babysitters Club, but instead of watching other kids, we looked out for one another and made sure that no matter where we were, we had a friend. The group was very diverse; we were different races, and we followed different religions. Our book club connected us. During lunch, we met with a teacher and discussed the book we were reading, but we'd often connect what we were reading to our personal lives. That was the glue that held us together.

Because we were so different, we had to rely on one another to understand the books because only a few of us lived the lives in the stories. I was able to learn about the different lives and religions of the world and of my friends, but the biggest takeaway for me was learning to respect all religions. I believe I was the only Christian in the friend group, but they always included me and respected my beliefs, and I did the same. Our friendship was strong because no matter where we were in life, we knew that the others were deserving of all the respect we could give.

Without knowing about others' lives and how to be respectful as a society, we will begin to move backward toward intolerance and hatred. Diversity resources open our eyes to the possibility of a world that respects all beliefs. It opens our eyes to see why it is so important to support other cultures and religions. I could have missed some of the greatest memories in my life and could have lost some of my best friends just by not knowing better. People argue that diversity resources are blasphemous but books such as *Let's Celebrate! Special Days Around the*

World by Kate DePalma and *Gratitude Is My Superpower* by Alicia Ortego highlight the best of every religion and teach children to love all people.

SECOND

Diversity resources about religion allow us to be seen.

Talks about religion and differences of religion weren't just a school conversation. Like many life lessons, these talks flowed over into the home as well. In Ohio, one of our neighbors, a family who had a different religion from my family's, was one of the best neighbors we have ever met. About six to seven moves and two different states later, we still stay in contact with the family, and when we visit Ohio, we often stop to visit them.

Part of the reason why we are so close to them is because my sister and I used to spend hours talking to their kids who were our age. Yes, we were brought up to not converse about religion and politics, but our little curious middle school minds couldn't resist. They used to invite us over to their swing set, and we'd sit and swing and talk about their faith versus ours. They are Muslim and believe in different prophets and have a different religious text than we have, but that didn't stop us from sharing our faiths.

None of us changed what we believed. We had the opportunity to share our faith in a safe environment. We all walked away feeling more connected with our religion and with a stronger faith in it because we felt seen. We respected one another. We were able to express ourselves and have the conversation that we all wanted to have despite having been taught that discussing it would lead to nothing but conflict and loss. The kids who don't have the opportunity to have those conversations need diversity resources to help them feel seen. Children can connect to their religion and to people through books and literature. It's not blasphemous to learn about others. Having the conversation about different faiths and religions allows us to open up about our beliefs and find a way to have important conversations without fighting and without hurting others. We need to move forward. Understanding one another and the ways we all think helps us to make the advancements needed so that the next generations will have the space to be who they are.

PART 2

Olivia Pituch, secretary and social media adviser for PARU

THIRD

Diversity is the opposite of being anti-religious.

Diversity by definition is "the practice or quality of including or involving people from a range of different social and ethnic backgrounds and of different genders, sexual orientations, etc." An alternate definition is "the state of being diverse; variety." Diversity is a natural part of humanity. Every human is different. What confuses me is the idea that diversity is "anti-religious."

To be anti-religious, according to *Merriam-Webster's Dictionary,* is to be "opposing or hostile to religion or to the power and influence of organized religion." Diversity is the opposite. A quick comparison of the definitions alone can tell you that. The concept of diversity allows exploration and education on every religion as well as the lack of religion.

I believe that many who think that diversity is anti-religious might not fully understand what it means to be anti-religious. Over the years, especially with the start of my activism, I have loved exploring diversity resources. This includes movies, books, TikTok accounts, YouTube videos, documentaries, and so much more. No diversity resources that I have encountered have been hostile toward religion. They have educated me on a variety of religions and experiences.

The concept that diversity resources are anti-religious almost implies that discussing or educating oneself on other religions is anti-religious. It implies that only certain religions are normal or correct, which is not true. Educating people on all religions promotes acceptance and understanding. It is natural to be more accepting of things you understand. To be able to learn about, understand, and embrace religion is so beautiful. Although I am no longer religious, I adore learning about different cultures and different religions. I find it fascinating and beautifully human to believe in higher powers and devote yourself to them.

This argument is also interesting because many diversity resources don't even touch on religion. There can be no hostility toward it because it is not mentioned. Some resources are simply educating people on protective hairstyles or foods in a certain culture. Resources that celebrate all cultures, identities, religions, and places should exist within education, especially when there is diversity within schools.

Diversity is loving, accepting, and educational. It allows others to learn and expand and grow. It allows the exploration of different concepts. It embraces and celebrates cultures, identities, and individual uniqueness.

WHAT TO SAY

When faced with the question of whether or not diversity resources are anti-religious, respond this way:

- **Books about different religions teach us how to respect one another.**
- **Diversity resources about religion allow us to be seen.**
- **Diversity is the opposite of being anti-religious.**

CHAPTER 14

IS IT WRONG TO SHOW NONTRADITIONAL FAMILIES AND LIFESTYLES?

Christina Ellis, vice president of PARU, 2021–2022

This world is a vast, beautiful, and scary place with wondrous mountains, breathtaking rivers, and unforgettable valleys. Yet it's frightening due to the world's hate, anger, and betrayal. I wonder why the nation is divided about books that promote such qualities as diversity, love, freedom, and self-expression. The books being banned around the nation tend to be elementary- and high-school-level books that highlight and celebrate the uniqueness of humanity. Parents and community members across the nation have expressed concern for diverse books within classrooms—saying the books aren't fit for students. Some districts such as the Central York School District placed bans on diverse materials. One of the major claims against diverse books is that they promote nontraditional families and lifestyles. Here are three rebuttals against that:

FIRST

The United States is a free country protected by the First Amendment.

Just about every time I talk about books being banned, there is at least one counterargument saying diverse books are not what America's founding fathers would have wanted. But I disagree. The reason why the thirteen colonies were established was that British citizens who felt smothered by the British government moved to the Americas to start new lives built on freedom of expression. Colonists eventually fought for independence from the British government, laying out their values in the Declaration of Independence and, later, in the US Constitution. I believe they meant it when they said, "We the People." Despite the persistence of segregation and discrimination, we as a nation have made progress to truly represent all the people of the United States. There is still more work to do. I believe the founding fathers, who went to great trouble to achieve liberty for themselves and to have their own voices heard, are best honored by continuing that work.

I remember, as a student, having to do a school project about my heritage and where I'm from. My teacher at the time brought us students to the school library to pick out books to use for the project. My classmates were flying through the shelves picking book after book about where they are from and who their parents are. I could only find two or three books that resonated with me. I had to go to

The students of PARU gather outside the Central York High School in August 2021 for one of their first protests.

the public library to find the books that fit my story the best. The feeling of excitement being overtaken by sudden disappointment is one I will never forget. I wish I got to experience the joy of finding books in my school library that fit my life and was able to share the joy among my peers. Marginalized students should be able to walk into their schools' libraries and find more than one or two books about their heritage. The founding fathers gave America freedom of speech, expression, assembly, and more. No parent or group should take that away.

SECOND

Public schools should not only highlight a certain way of living but should educate their students in an unbiased manner. Private schools are available for families and students who value certain identities. I believe a public school should be where all learners are welcome. A public school should be free of religious, governmental, and political affiliations and should be where all learners feel they matter, regardless of their background.

More important, families look different for each individual. Many students need the mom, dad, sibling, and pet kind of family. Some students have parents who are divorced, foster or adopted parents, extended family members who raise them, two moms, two dads, or nonbinary or transgender parents or guardians. The combinations of how a family can look are endless. Schools should not just praise a stereotypical, "traditional" family and shy away from highlighting other ways a family can look. Growing and developing in school can be hard. As a student, you are learning from books, but you are also learning about yourself and how you fit into the world and about the people around you. I hope this nation doesn't make students feel uncomfortable about the people they love because their household doesn't look "correct" to certain people. It shouldn't matter who the students look up to as their parental figures as long as the parental figure is treating the student correctly and raising them to be a responsible member of society. It is none of our business.

There are many traditions and religions all over the world, but none of them are incorrect. The last part of the claim that these books are anti-religious was very bold, especially when talking about public schools. America is not a religious-affiliated country; America does not have a national religion, as we have freedom of expression covered by the First Amendment. Why are parents and community members complaining about diverse books that don't promote religion? Public schools should offer a well-rounded education. It *can* include learning about different religions around the world. This shouldn't scare parents as it is a part of learning. This society will not survive if kids are sheltered into only knowing their way of life. There will be little empathy, understanding, and compassion for others in this world. Parents are urging schools to provide an unbiased education yet only want one religious view to be taught. Isn't this contradictory?

Students who do not practice the Western predominant religions within the United States need to be considered. This is America with the freedom of expression. It is not the place for public schools to tell students what religion they should practice. That is a personal matter.

Books that highlight the wondrous and beautiful diversity of this world are being put on the chopping block in many parts of the United States. There have been claims that diverse books are promoting nontraditional families and are anti-religious. But America is a country built on the foundation of democracy and choice. If a personal choice an American makes isn't negatively impacting them or others, it should not be of concern to others.

THIRD

Families come in all different kinds. It is not the place of fellow community members to tell another family that their family is wrong. As long as students are being cared for, it should not matter who their parents are. And it is not the place of schools to shun kids who have what society calls nontraditional families.

There are many different religions, and no student should feel isolated because theirs is not commonly known or practiced among their peers. Schools should be a safe place to learn and grow, which includes learning about other cultures, religions, and ways of life. It would be sad to see America, which prides itself on being the land of the free, silence the voices and expressions of citizens.

In my activism with PARU, I have shared my story of feeling isolated at times during my K–12 schooling as an African Caribbean American student. School should be where all learners feel they belong and are supported in their growth. Just because a few parents don't agree with other students' personal way of life does not mean schools should make district-wide decisions to silence different religions and different ways families are structured. The founding fathers took steps to create a democratic country so citizens could express who they are. Then throughout the years and decades, America has made steps to make sure that *all* people are respected and represented in government and society. I would be sad to see America take steps back because a handful of people are terrified of the change the country is trying to make.

WHAT TO SAY

When faced with the question of whether or not it's wrong to show nontraditional families and lifestyles, respond this way:

- **The United States is a free country protected by the First Amendment.**
- **Public schools should not highlight only one way of living but should educate their students in an unbiased manner.**
- **Families come in all different kinds.**

CONCLUSION

NO MORE APOLOGIES FOR A BLEEDING HEART WHEN THE OPPOSITE IS NO HEART AT ALL. DANGER OF LOSING OUR HUMANITY MUST BE MET WITH MORE HUMANITY.

—TONI MORRISON

As this book was going to print, the Department of Education, under the second Trump administration, announced plans to dismiss eleven outstanding complaints against book bans—calling them "a hoax"—and moved to eliminate the position of book ban coordinator at the Office for Civil Rights.

This book serves as a living record of book bans in our local community. It was real when our school board voted to eliminate the use of over four hundred books and resources by and about Black, brown, and LGBTQIA+ authors. It was very real when an email was sent to all staff saying that we "are not permitted to utilize" these materials in the classroom and to "double check that none of these resources are being used." PARU did not go out to protest and share our stories at board meetings for a hoax.

Currently book bans are on the rise across the country. In the 2023–2024 school year, PEN America counted more than ten thousand book bans in public schools in twenty-nine different states over 220 school districts. The truth remains: Book bans are a very clear and present danger to the intellectual freedoms guaranteed to all Americans.

Ban This! was written to equip readers to understand and implement the arguments and counterarguments PARU used in our fight against the book bans in our district. It is our hope that you, the reader, will take these counterarguments and bring them back into your communities and utilize them to address misinformation at your school board meetings, at your dining room tables, in social media posts, or in grocery aisle interactions. Share them. Refuse to be gaslit about the actual truth.

We hope you read this book and are inspired to move past performative allyship to active participation in the freedom struggle. We need coconspirators—people who are willing to step out of the arena seats and into the trenches in the fight for intellectual freedom and social justice. We cannot waste any more time. As Bettina Love puts it: "The time is past due" to get into this fight.

So, what will it be for you? What are you now going to do with the new information you gained from this book? Will you commit to not just speak your truth but to speak your truth to power? Will you decide to spend any privilege you may have in order to amplify and elevate the marginalized voices around you? Will you stop playing it safe on the sidelines and step into the arena?

On the back of every PARU shirt is a powerful challenge from the late American hero John Lewis: "When you see something that is not right, not just, you have a moral obligation to do something." Perhaps this can be your mantra too: to go out into your community and do something about the unfair and unjust situations that exist.

So don't let this opportunity go to waste. Coretta Scott King said that "freedom is never really won. You earn it and win it in every generation." May this be your call to go out and win freedom for YOUR generation and those who follow.

APPENDIX

Sapphire, the author of *Push*, which appeared on the banned books list, sent a statement to the board, read by Patricia A. Jackson:

Dear Fellow Citizen Readers and Writers:

We enter hollow ground covering unseen sinkholes when we ban works of art. Decades ago, academics moaned over the "closing of the American mind". When we ban books like *Push*, *The Color Purple*, *Beloved*, and *The Autobiography of Malcolm X*, we stand not just to close our collective minds, but to lose them. We've entered into an age where the inability to feel and empathize has led to a collective psychosis characterized by mass murders in the classroom and in our places of worship.

Push is a book about the awakening and healing of a violent and violated child. Through acts of love demonstrated by her teacher and classmates she becomes an academic success story and a proud loving mother. *Push* is a story about the power of language, the letters of the alphabet, that many of our children leave school never having learned. *Push* is about the power of language to transform and open the mind and the heart. *Push* heals, *Push* teaches, but most of all *Push* loves. When we ban books like *Push*, we are in danger of falling into the sinkholes of hate and prejudice and ignorance, and of losing what little love we have left for each other.

Yours in healing, hope and love,

Sapphire

SOURCE NOTES

12 "Precisely at the . . . with your society": James Baldwin, "A Talk to Teachers," *The Saturday Review*, December 21, 1963, 42–44.

21 "Do we even have a race problem here?": "CYSD Board Meeting 7-20-2020," YouTube video, 56:21, CYSD Board Minutes, August 10, 2020, https://youtu.be/-U1PgntH7FI?si=rogYW78jQ4XjQQDk.

30 "Mirror books provide . . . they can be.": Tracey Flores, DSandra Osorio, and Colorín Colorado, "Why Diverse Books Matter: Mirrors and Windows," Colorín Colorado, accessed May 13, 2025, https://www.colorincolorado.org/article/why-diverse-books-matter-mirrors-and-windows.

31 "Microaggressions are the . . . form of behavior": "How to Combat Microaggressions with Derald Wing Sue, PhD," *Speaking of Psychology*, podcast, American Psychology Association, accessed August 2023, https://www.apa.org/news/podcasts/speaking-of-psychology/microaggressions.

33 "More than half . . . adult in the home.": CDC, "New CDC Data Illuminate Youth Mental Health Threats During the COVID-19 Pandemic," news release, March 31, 2022, https://archive.cdc.gov/www_cdc_gov/media/releases/2022/p0331-youth-mental-health-covid-19.html.

34 "academic learning are . . . ability to learn": Jessica Souza, "What Is Social and Emotional Learning?," Child Mind Institute, updated February 4, 2025, https://childmind.org/article/what-is-social-and-emotional-learning/.

35 "When people read . . . another person's perspective.": Jason Pache, "Why Should We Read?," *Telescope*, May 21, 2023, https://the-telescope.com/1012/impact-magazine/spring-2023/why-should-we-read/.

45–46 Diversity education helps uncover biases: Mary E. Kite and Patricia Clark, "The Benefits of Diversity Education," American Psychological Association, September 8, 2022, https://www.apa.org/ed/precollege/psychology-teacher-network/introductory-psychology/benefits-of-diversity.

46 Helping students having difficult conversations: Kite and Clark.

51 "A book ban . . . or a district.": Kanopi_admin, "What Is a Book Ban? And More Frequently Asked Questions," PEN America, September 19, 2022, https://pen.org/book-bans-frequently-asked-questions/.

51–52 "The fact that . . . just a coincidence,": Evan McMorris-Santoro, Linh Tran, Sahar Akbarzai, and Mirna Alsharif, "Students Fight Back Against a Book Ban That Has a Pennsylvania Community Divided," CNN, September 16, 2021, https://www.cnn.com/2021/09/15/us/book-ban-controversy-pennsylvania/index.html?cid=ios_app.

58 "The ruin of . . . in its homes.": Robert Anderson, *Elements of Literature: Second Course* (Holt, Rinehart and Winston, 1989), 126.

59 "Love your neighbor as yourself.": Lev. 19:18.

59 "not every human . . . of my child's empathy.": "'Not Every Human Is Deserving of My Child's Empathy'; West Shore School District Sued," CBS 21, updated

February 10, 2023, https://local21news.com/news/crisis-in-the-classroom/parents-sue-west-shore-school-district-for-new-character-strong-curriculum.

61 "When we ban . . . for each other.": Sapphire, letter to Central York School Board, March 27, 2023.

64 "Allyship is not . . . practice allyship consistently.": Layra Saad, *Me and White Supremacy* (Sourcebooks, 2023), 126.

71 "I love America . . . criticize her perpetually.": "CYSD Board Meeting 7-20-2020."

71 "to make America . . . a better nation.": James Baldwin, *Notes of a Native Son* (Beacon, 1955), 54.

73 "The purpose of . . . something about it.": Saad, *Me and White Supremacy*, 83.

75 "I want to . . . action is meaningless.": Saad, 47.

78 Diversity resources help students: Jeremy Adam Smith, "How Students Benefit from School Diversity," *Greater Good Magazine*, August 15, 2017, https://greatergood.berkeley.edu/article/item/how_students_benefit_from_school_diversity.

94 "Between January 1 . . . documented by ALA": "Book Ban Data," American Library Association, accessed March 30, 2024, https://www.ala.org/bbooks/book-ban-data.

94–95 "47% of the books . . . LGBTQIA+ and BIPOC individuals": Unite Against Book Bans, accessed March 30, 2024, https://uniteagainstbookbans.org/2023-book-bans/.

95–96 "the United States' . . . challenged that power.": "What You Need to Know About the Book Bans Sweeping the U.S.," Teachers College, Columbia University, September 2023, https://www.tc.columbia.edu/articles/2023/september/what-you-need-to-know-about-the-book-bans-sweeping-the-us.

96 "remorse or shame . . . inequality and injustice.": *Oxford English Dictionary,* "white guilt," accessed June 25, 2024, https://www.oed.com/dictionary/white-guilt_n.

104 "high-quality academic . . . passions and interests.": "District," Central York School District, accessed August 4, 2023, https://www.cysd.k12.pa.us/our-district.

105 A 2022 survey by the National Education Association: Tim Walker, "Survey: Alarming Number of Educators May Soon Leave the Profession," NEA Today, February 1, 2022, https://www.nea.org/nea-today/all-news-articles/survey-alarming-number-educators-may-soon-leave-profession.

107 Youth mental health statistics: "Teen Mental Health Facts and Statistics 2024," Compass Health Center, updated March 17, 2025, https://compasshealthcenter.net.

111–112 Eva, discussion with author, May 2022.

113 "The purpose of . . . his own decisions.": James Baldwin, "A Talk to Teachers," *The Saturday Review,* December 21, 1963, 42–44.

114 "get over themselves . . . is just hard.": "Board Curriculum Committee 4-11-22,"YouTube video, 41:13, CYSD Board Minutes, April 22, 2022, https://youtu.be/x7QQyfFziiE?feature=shared.

116 The precedent for defining pornography for both federal and state law: *Miller v. California* 413 U.S. 15 (1973).

138 "the practice or . . . genders, sexual orientations, etc.": *Oxford English Dictionary*, "diversity," accessed July 10, 2024, https://www.oed.com/dictionary/diversity_n.

138 "the state of being diverse; variety.": *Dictionary.com*, "diversity," accessed July 10, 2024, https://www.dictionary.com/browse/diversity.

139 "opposing or hostile . . . of organized religion.": *Merriam-Webster Dictionary*, "anti-religious," accessed July 10, 2024, https://www.merriam-webster.com/dictionary/anti-religious.

148 "No more apologies . . . with more humanity.": Toni Morrison, *The Source of Self-Regard* (Knopf, 2019), 105.

148 "none of these . . . are being used.": Ryan Caufman, email to author, August 11, 2021.

149 "the time is past due": Bettina Love, RESI Keynote Speech at Columbia University, 2021.

150 "When you see . . . situations that exist.": John Lewis, Speech at University of Washington, February 2017.

150 "Freedom is never . . . in every generation.": Coretta Scott King, *My Life with Dr. Martin Luther King Jr.* (Henry Holt, 1993), 79.

152 "Dear Fellow Citizens . . . and love, Sapphire.": Sapphire, letter.

FURTHER RESOURCES

Anderson, Elijah. *Black in White Space: The Enduring Impact of Color in Everyday Life*. University of Chicago Press, 2023. Anderson sheds fresh light on the dire persistence of racial discrimination in our country.

Baldwin, James. "A Talk to Teachers," 1963. https://www.zinnedproject.org/materials/baldwin-talk-to-teachers. Baldwin gave this seminal speech to teachers to help them understand HOW to better connect with Black children in classroom settings.

Jones-Rogers, Stephanie E. *They Were Her Property: White Women as Slave Owners in the American South*. Yale University Press, 2020. This is a bold and searing investigation into the role of white women in the American slave economy.

Joseph, Peniel E. *The Sword and the Shield: The Revolutionary Lives of Malcolm X and Martin Luther King Jr*. Basic Books, 2021. This dual biography of Malcolm X and Martin Luther King Jr. helps our understanding of the twentieth century's most iconic African American leaders.

King, Jr., Martin Luther. *Where Do We Go from Here: Chaos or Community*. Beacon Press, 2010. King's final book where he lays out his plans and dreams for America.

Morrison, Toni. *The Source of Self-Regard*. Knopf, 2019. This is a collection of Morrison's most vital speeches and essays from over forty years of work.

Saad, Layla. *Me and White Supremacy: Combat Racism, Change the World and Become a Good Ancestor*. Sourcebooks, 2023. This book challenges the white readers to unpack white supremacist notions and biases while encouraging them to take action as an anti-racist.

INDEX

ACKNOWLEDGMENTS

- Pennsylvania State Education Association—for recognizing the work of PARU with the Adler Human and Civil Rights Award
- Matt Fargen and Lauri Lebo of the Pennsylvania State Education Association for their protection and advocacy in the fight
- Vic Walczak of the American Civil Liberties Union for keeping two good teachers on the job against all odds
- Dr. Bettina Love for defining our activism as the work of twenty-first-century abolition and reminding us that the time to fight is "past due"
- Jose Vilson for his sage support and nudging us to write this story down for future generations
- Charlyn Henderson for being a lightning rod of hope, a calming presence, and a catalyst for connecting us to legends behind the freedom struggle
- Brad Meltzer for speaking truth to power directly in the Central York board room and reminding us to not let the extremists own the definition of patriotism
- Hannah Shipley for taking up the fight on TikTok, delivering the message, and distributing four thousand books to a grateful community in fifteen minutes
- Ruby Martin, YWCA, for sheltering PARU when their own district would not and allowing us a safe place for multiple interviews

- Dr. Andrea Berry, superintendent of the School District of the City of York, for also sheltering PARU and allowing us a safe place for an interview with Representative Malcolm Kenyatta
- Tina Locurto, *York Dispatch* reporter, for uplifting our voice (deserves a Pulitzer for her reporting on this incident)
- Dr. Bernice King for the courage and persistence to continue her father's work to create the Beloved Community
- Dr. Kelisha Graves and the King Center for recognizing the work of PARU during the book banning and awarding them the Beloved Community Award, Youth Influencer as well as offering free training in the Nonviolence365 program
- Jonathan Friedman and Kasey Meehan of PEN America for uplifting our story, providing breakfast to PARU during the protests, and offering refuge and resources to continue the fight
- Kelly Jensen and Book Riot for amplifying PARU's story and their tireless advocacy against book bans across the country
- Dr. Michael S. Snell for risking it all against the odds to do the right thing for the students and the community of the Central York School District
- Amanda and Jamie Hill for keeping the most accurate records at the board meetings and holding the board members accountable for their words and deeds, even when those same board members tried to change narrative
- Julie Womack of Red Wine and Blue for recognizing the work of PARU and giving them the opportunity to bring their story before the United States Congress

- Ryan Caufman, who bore the brunt of a decision that was not his and still held the line.
- Samantha Schlundt and Michael Mountz for the supportive texts and late night phone calls
- All the kids of PARU . . . all generations, particularly the first generation—Princess Gabriel, Aly Sergeon, Layla Smith, and Unique Fields
- Sara Megibow, who asked the simplest of questions and then stepped in to be our tireless protector and the agent of the century

ABOUT THE AUTHORS

CHRISTINA ELLIS is blessed to have been able to dedicate her life to serving and advocating for others. She began her life of advocacy in high school and through higher education continues to advocate within the community of the university she attends. Her dedication to seeing the world as a more equitable place has led her to the career of medicine. As a scientist, she advocates for minorities within the scientific field and hopes to continue to advocate to break barriers of those of marginalized communities. *Ban This! How One School Fought Two Book Bans and Won (and How You Can Too)* is Ellis's first book. She is excited to have been given this opportunity to share her story alongside her coauthors!

RENEE ELLIS is fueled by her passion for finding beauty in the world and the people around her. She began her activism in high school and continues to advocate for diversity, equity, and inclusion while pursuing higher education. Ellis is also dedicated to empowering students to engage in politics and exercise their right to vote. This commitment to social change complements her interests in creative direction, fashion, and art. As an artist and designer, she integrates her advocacy into her artistic endeavors, striving to use art and design to uplift her community and support others. *Ban This! How One School Fought Two Book Bans and Won (and How You Can Too)* is Ellis's first book, and she is proud to present this work alongside the students and teachers who were also involved in this passion project!

EDHA GUPTA is a twenty-year-old activist who served as the president of the Panther Anti-Racist Union during the 2021–2022 school year. Gupta, fellow officers, and advisers successfully protested a school board decision to ban over three hundred books on diversity education throughout the Central York School District. Through activism and advocacy, Gupta worked with her peers to promote diversity and inclusion in their school and community. By sharing the power of her story as an Indian American, Gupta hopes to inspire young activists to make a difference through impactful change, resulting in memorable and long-lasting change in education and throughout the country. Gupta has cofounded an organization named EmpowerED with Christina Ellis, Renee Ellis, and Olivia Pituch, with the mission to aid students across the country who are combating similar attacks on their education. She is also a student at the University of Pittsburgh majoring in neuroscience minoring in sociology, and she hopes to advocate for equity in medicine in her future.

BEN HODGE is a twenty-plus-year veteran of the classroom and stage. He teaches acting and speech classes and serves as the artistic director for his high school. He has directed over fifty productions, and his play *Reach* was performed off-Broadway in 2009. A passionate advocate for education policy and diversity initiatives, he created the Panther Anti-Racist Union in 2020 to establish a space for students to have courageous conversations and advocacy regarding social justice issues. This group went on to overturn two book bans in their district. When he is not teaching or advocating, he is reading history, gaming, or binge-watching shows with his wife, two teenage children, and two Yorkies.

PATRICIA A. JACKSON is a thirty-one-year veteran in secondary education. She teaches world literature and creative writing at a high school in south-central Pennsylvania. When the school board voted to ban hundreds of books based on race and sexual orientation, she joined the Panther Anti-Racist Union as a co-adviser to assist the successful fight to overturn that ruling. A published author, she enjoys writing urban fantasy and occasionally dabbles in the Star Wars universe.

OLIVIA PITUCH is a twenty-year-old activist and a member of the LGBTQAI+ community. Along with her fellow authors, Olivia organized multiple protests that led to the reversal of a book ban instituted by the district school board, which removed more than three hundred books on diversity. She is now a third-year student at Elizabethtown College and plans to continue the fight for diversity and representation by majoring in the field of political science and dual minoring in women and gender studies and psychology. Her passion for music, philosophy, reading, education, and art has made her the person she is today, and she hopes to continue uplifting and empowering the voices of the youth to enact positive change. Diversity is not a threat.

PHOTO ACKNOWLEDGMENTS

Image credits: Courtesy of the authors, pp. 15, 55, 101; Kerem Yücel/Minnesota Public Radio via AP, p. 18; Todd Strand/Alamy, p. 19; iSidhe/Getty Images, p. 23; Courtesy of PEN America, pp. 32, 33; hamdi bendali/Shutterstock, pp. 40, 130; Paras Griffin/Getty Images for Paramount+, p. 41; © Shelly Stallsmith – USA TODAY NETWORK via Imagn Images, p. 66; Andrew Toth/Getty Images for Columbia Pictures, p. 80; julio donoso/Sygma via Getty Images, p. 114; Patti McConville/Alamy, p. 122; Couresty of Ben Hodge, p. 143. Design elements: Buzaeva Valeriia/Shutterstock; Krakenimages.com/Shutterstock.